First Sewing

First published in the United Kingdom in 2014 by
Collins & Brown
10 Southcombe Street
London
W14 0RA

An imprint of Anova Books Company Ltd

Distributed in the US and Canada by Sterling Publishing Co, Inc.
387 Park Avenue South, New York, NY 10016-8810

5413 2682

5/14

ISBN 978-1-909397-16-3

A CIP catalogue for this book is available from the British Library.

10 9 8 7 6 5 4 3 2 1

Reproduction by Rival
Printed by 1010 Printing International Ltd, China

This book can be ordered direct from the publisher at
www.anovabooks.com

Photographers by Holly Jolliffe (pages 7, 11, 43, 46, 48–49, 50–53,
60–61, 78–81, 82 and 84–85); Kristin Perers (pages 6, 16, 56–57, 58–59,
62, 72–75 and 76–77); Michael Wicks (pages 8, 9, 11, 13, 15, 42 and 45);
Christina Wilson (pages 54–55, 64–67, 68–71, 86–89, 90–93, 94–97,
98–101, 102, 104· 107, 108–111, 112–115 and 116–119).

Illustrations by Kuo Kang Chen and Barking Dog Art.

Acknowledgements

The publisher would like to thank Maggi McCormick Gordon,
Marie Clayton, Lena Santana, Rebecca Shreeve and Nicki Trench.
Thank you also to Kuo Kang Chen for the techniques illustrations and to
Janome UK for supplying the sewing machine.

First Sewing

Simple projects for beginners

COLLINS & BROWN

Contents

WORKSHOP
16

SIMPLE STITCHING
46

Apron
48

Shopper
50

Basic Cushion
54

Shoulder Bag
56

Lace Bow Top
58

Patchwork Blanket
60

SHAPING AND
FASTENING
62

Olivia the Sheep
64

Doggy Draught
Excluder
68

Simple Skirt
72

How to use this book

Sewing is a wonderful skill that will open up a whole new world of creative opportunities. The basics are really easy to learn, and even things that may seem more complex are often quite easy to tackle if you break them down into smaller sections.

One of the major advantages of being able to sew is that you can choose your own fabrics and colours to make a range of coordinated items that are different from the standard ones offered in the shops. And when you understand how things are constructed and have learned some basic skills, you will be able to repair most damaged or worn fabric items, or recycle them into something new and different.

Things to consider

- Your skill level and time available – if you are inexperienced, don't be too ambitious to begin with. It's better to stitch a simple item perfectly than to produce a complicated one badly, or to try to make something in too much of a rush so it is not finished well.
- Fabric choices – there is a wide range of fabric available and choosing the right one for your item can make the difference between success and failure. Always try to use the same type of fabric as given in a project, although the colour or pattern you choose is entirely up to you.
- Embellishing ready-made items is a quick and easy way to create something unique if you have limited time.

This book is divided into sections. First we have Getting Started, which details basic sewing equipment and covers some information about different fabrics. Workshop covers all the stitching skills you need to make the projects in the book. Each of the techniques is numbered and the same reference number is given in the project whenever the technique appears so you can quickly refer back if you need to. The remaining part of the book has four sections: Simple Stitching, which has projects that are fast and easy to make to get you started; Shaping and Fastening, which looks at making slightly more complex shapes and tries out different fastening methods; Embellishing, using embroidery, appliqué, and adding trims and borders; and finally Extending Skills, which has a collection of bigger projects that are still reasonably simple but that will take longer and will put into practice some of the more advanced techniques.

Filled with many exciting projects illustrated with helpful step-by-step instructions, this book is all you need to discover the joys of stitching.

Getting started

Many projects can be made with hand stitching alone so there is no need to invest in expensive equipment, such as a sewing machine, until you are sure you want to take things further – although if you do, a machine will make stitching long seams much faster and easier. It is worth buying good-quality basic equipment; this section covers the essential items you will need.

Equipment

Erasable markers

Ideal to mark fabric for embroidery or to transfer any type of marking from a pattern or template. The marks from water-erasable markers are sponged away with water, so they may not be suitable for fabric that cannot be washed. The marks from air-erasable markers fade over time, so they may not be suitable for projects that will take a long time to complete. Test markers on scrap fabric first to make sure the marks show up and can be removed successfully.

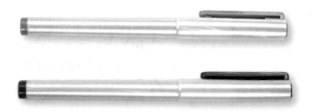

Stranded embroidery thread (floss)

This type of decorative thread (floss) is available in a wide range of colours and is made up of six strands twisted together. It can be used as it is for a thicker line, or one or more strands can be separated out for a finer stitch.

Dressmaker's chalk

Solid chalk for marking fabric often comes in a triangular shape for ease of use and to make a range of line thicknesses.

Pincushion

There is a wide range of pincushions available, so experiment and find what works best for you. A popular choice is the kind with an elastic strap that can be worn on the wrist, literally keeping your pins close at hand.

Thimble

Many people do not like thimbles, but their fingers sure do! If you do a lot of sewing you will soon get accustomed to the way a thimble feels.

Thread

Thread comes in a range of fibres – both natural and synthetic – and colours. It also comes in different thicknesses for a variety of purposes. Thicker threads are normally used for techniques like topstitching, where the stitches are visible as part of the design.

Dressmaker's scissors

These have blades at an angle to the handles, so the blade can slide along the work surface when cutting without lifting the fabric much. This allows for more accurate cutting.

Tape measure

A flexible tape measure is useful to take measurements of the body or any three-dimensional item.

Embroidery scissors

The short, shaped blades of embroidery scissors are designed to trim threads. Do not use your dressmaker's scissors for this, as it can eventually blunt the blades.

Tracing wheel and dressmaker's carbon

This is the quickest way to transfer continuous lines. The dressmaker's carbon is placed between the pattern and the fabric, and the tracing wheel is run along the lines to transfer lines of dots to the fabric.

Glass-headed pins

The large, coloured heads of these pins brighten up your sewing and make them easy to spot when you need to remove them. Choose glass heads over plastic, which may melt if caught with an iron.

Needles

From left to right: sharps (ordinary sewing needle available in several sizes); darner (long needle for darning and basting); small-eyed embroidery (for fine embroidery yarn); large-eyed embroidery (for thicker embroidery yarn); tapestry (blunt with a large eye for canvas fabric and threading ribbon or thin elastic); sewing machine needle (available in a variety of sizes and shapes for different uses).

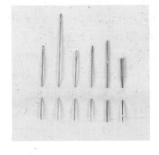

Sewing machine

This is an expensive piece of equipment, so take the time to be sure you buy one you enjoy using. Borrow one to make your first couple of projects – this will give you some idea of which functions you need and which ones are extras. Try out different machines in the showroom and take advantage of any instruction that may be offered. The instruction book will cover your specific machine, but most machines share some basic common features.

Threading the machine

Follow the threading guide to take the thread end from the reel, through the guide eyes and tensioning wheel and down to the needle. Turn the hand wheel to position the needle above the plate. Insert the thread through the eye of the needle from front to back. Pull the end through, leaving it long enough to pull to the back and secure under the foot when you begin to sew. Always thread the sewing machine with the presser foot raised.

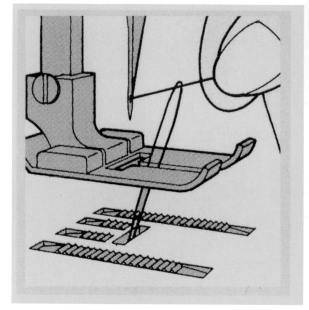

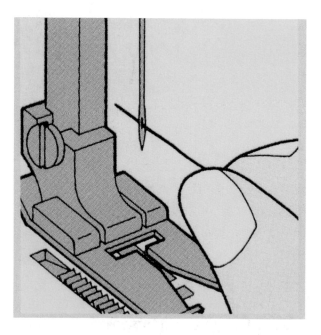

Pulling up the bobbin thread

Check the manual to see which way round to insert the bobbin into its case, then pull the end of the thread through the tension spring on the case and leave it hanging free. Make sure the needle is threaded correctly, then turn the hand wheel once holding on to the end of the top thread. The top thread should catch the bottom thread and pull a loop up through the plate. Pull gently on the loop to bring the bottom thread end through.

Thread tension

Both top and bottom thread are held under tension as the machine stitches; to achieve a perfect seam the tension should be the same on both sides. Modern machines often have automatic tension regulators, but older machines may need to be adjusted by hand. This is usually done by adjusting the top tension – most manufacturers recommend leaving the bottom tension alone, although it may be possible to adjust it in extreme cases by turning a screw in the bobbin case. To check the tension is correct, stitch a seam on a scrap of the fabric you are using.

Balanced stitch

If the tension is correct, the line of stitching will look exactly the same on both sides, because the two threads cross over right in the middle of the fabric layers being stitched.

Top thread too loose

Here the bottom thread is a straight line and the top thread comes through the fabric to show on the back. Tighten the top tension to resolve this.

Top thread too tight

Here the top thread is a straight line and the bottom thread is showing on the front. Loosen the top tension to resolve this.

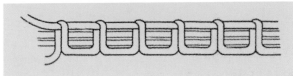

Machine presser foot

The presser foot holds the fabric firmly against the plate while the stitch is formed. The foot can be changed and there are many types available for different functions. Your sewing machine will come with basic alternatives; this will be all you need to begin with, but later you might want to purchase one of the special feet if you are doing a lot of a particular type of work.

Using the machine

Sewing machines have a small built-in light that creates a bright working area. Replace the bulb immediately if it burns out, as insufficient light increases the risk of eyestrain or accidental injury.

Use your machine regularly, even for small tasks, to become familiar with it.

Check the manual to see if you need to carry out minor maintenance tasks, such as adding a drop of oil or cleaning the bobbin case. Attention to this will save on repair bills in the long term.

There are different machine needles for different tasks, just as in hand sewing. Make sure you select the correct needle for the fabric you are working with.

Zip foot

Ideal for putting zips in neatly and also useful for inserting piping into a seam. The narrow foot slides down the side of the zip teeth or piping and you can usually adjust the foot so you can stitch along either side. Some types are wider but have a groove underneath that slides over the zip teeth/piping.

Rolled hem foot

This has a curled piece of metal at the front that turns under the edge of lightweight and medium fabric to create a rolled hem as you stitch.

Pintuck foot

The ridges on the underside of this foot pull the fabric into a series of small tucks, which can then be stitched in neatly.

Darning/quilting/embroidery/appliqué foot

This has a small round or C-shaped end so very little of the stitching area is obscured. It is often used with the feed dog (the teeth that move the fabric along) disengaged for greater control of stitching direction.

Understanding fabrics

There are a wide variety of different types of fabric available, in both natural and synthetic yarns, but some factors are common to ranges of fabric, such as structure – woven, knitted, or non-woven – and available widths. If you are using patterned fabric or one with a pile or nap, you also need to be aware of pattern repeats and the direction of the raised surface, and take these into account when purchasing fabric and planning your project.

Woven fabrics

These are made up of two sets of yarn: the warp and the weft. The warp runs lengthwise in the loom; the weft runs widthwise at right angles to the warp. Woven fabrics are made in different patterns by taking the weft thread over and under the warp in different sequences. The selvedge is the border down both edges of a length of woven fabric – it is often woven more tightly and may pucker when the fabric is cleaned so it is usually discarded for sewing projects. The lengthwise and widthwise directions – or straight grains – of a woven fabric are firm so fabric has very little give in either of these directions. But if pulled diagonally, or on the bias grain, the fabric will stretch. True bias is at a 45-degree angle to the selvedge.

Knitted fabrics

All knitted fabrics are constructed using just one yarn running in the same direction and looping around itself. Warp knits have their yarn running along the length of the fabric, while weft knits have their yarn running across the width. Because of its construction, knitted fabric has some give in every direction, making it ideal for close-fitting garments. It is used less often for furnishings and accessories.

Non-woven fabrics

This category includes fabrics such as felt, interfacing, lace and net. Felt is made of compressed wool or wool/acrylic-mix fibre; it does not fray and can be moulded to a shape. Knitted fabrics can also be felted by being washed at high temperatures and then tumble-dried; this process is also known as fulling.

Interfacing is a compressed synthetic fabric used as a backing to the main fabric to give extra body, shaping and support. It can be either sown in or fusible so it can be applied with an iron.

Both lace and net are made of fine yarns knotted into intricate patterns with open spaces between the motifs as part of the design. They can be either machine-made or handmade.

Standard fabric widths

Fabrics are available in standard widths, but different types of fabric have different standards. For instance, printed cotton is usually 90cm (36in), 110cm (44in), or sometimes 137cm (54in) wide, but voiles for curtains may be 300cm (120in) wide, while pure silk may only be 45cm (18in). Some manufacturers weave in metric and some still in imperial, so conversions may not be exact. For instance, a fabric woven on a 36-inch loom may be labelled as being 90cm wide, but will actually be slightly wider.

45cm (18in)
90cm (36in)
110cm (44in)
112cm (45in)
115cm (46in)
137cm (54in)
140cm (55in)
150cm (60in)
300cm (120in)

Buying fabric

Measure the fabric width before purchasing if it is critical to your project.

Allow extra for matching if you are using a fabric with a pattern repeat, pile or nap. To estimate how much extra, see right.

Buy thread and fabric at the same time; it is easier to match the colour with the fabric at hand.

Pattern repeats

If you are using patterned fabric, particularly for curtains or duvet covers requiring several widths of fabric, you will need to match up the motifs across seams. In most patterns, whether woven or printed, the same motif will be repeated again and again down the length and across the width; the distance between each is called the repeat. The pattern repeat may be given in the fabric specification; if not, measure from the tip of one motif to the corresponding tip of the next along the length, or if it is a circular motif use an easily identifiable point in the design instead.

If the pattern repeat is small you might be able to match the design without additional fabric, but if it is large you need to calculate in multiples of the repeat.

Estimating fabric with repeats

Measure the length you need, divide this by the repeat, round the result up to the next full number, then multiply this by the repeat again to get the length you need in complete pattern repeats. For instance, if you are making curtains with a drop of 230cm (92in) and need 4 widths, with no repeat you need length of drop × number of widths = 920cm (368in) of fabric. However, say your pattern repeat is 35cm (14in). First divide the drop by the repeat to get the number of repeats: 230 divided by 35 = 6.57; round up to the nearest number = 7, then multiply the repeat by this number, so 35 × 7 = 245cm (644in). So each drop needs to be 245cm (98in) × 4 widths = 980cm (392in) of fabric.

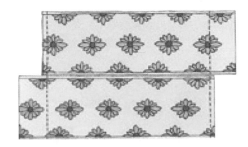

Nap and pile

These types of fabric have a raised surface and look lighter or darker depending on which way the light falls, or in which direction they are smoothed. With napped fabrics the short fibres have been brought to the surface and brushed in one direction, while pile fabric is woven with raised loops on the surface that are left as loops or cut into single threads.

The nap or pile should run in the same direction on each part of a garment or furnishing project, or it will look as if it has been made with two different colours of fabric (although this could also be utilized as part of the design). Dressmaking patterns give special cutting layouts with all pieces facing in one direction to allow for nap or pile, and will specify if an extra amount of fabric is required.

Wash and wear

Always check the laundering instructions on the fabric bolt when you purchase your fabric. Avoid mixing washable fabrics with those that must be drycleaned. If it is unavoidable, follow the care instructions for the most delicate fabric.

When choosing a lining fabric, choose a colour to tone with the main fabric or match one of the colours in the design.

Workshop

Use this section to learn all the basic
techniques you will need to make the
projects in this book, plus a few extras
that will be useful when you come to make
other sewing projects. It includes both
hand and machine stitching techniques,
all explained with step-by-step illustrations.

1 Threading the needle

Cut the thread with sharp scissors; it's much harder to thread with a ragged end. Hold the needle in the left hand and the thread in the right hand between thumb and index finger.

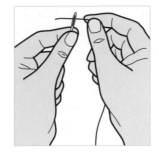

Pass the end of the thread through the eye of the needle and with the same motion pass the needle into the right hand and use the left hand to pull the thread through and down.

Quick knotting

The most common method to secure a length of thread before you begin stitching is to make a knot at the end. Hold the threaded needle in your right hand, pressing against the eye so the thread cannot slip out. Take the other end of the thread in your left hand and use your right hand to bring the thread right around the tip of the index finger to cross over the thread end. Use your left thumb to roll the loop off your finger into a knot.

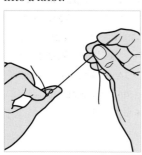

2 Tacking

Tacking or basting stitches are used to hold layers of fabric together temporarily until final stitching. The stitches can be quite long so they are fast to make and easy to remove when no longer needed.

1   Come up through the fabric at A, back down through it at B, then up to the surface again at C. Don't pull the thread through the fabric yet.

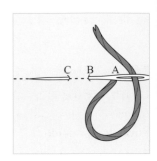

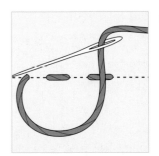

2   Continue by going back down through the fabric at D and coming up at E. Pull the thread through very gently to avoid causing gathers in the fabric.

3   Keep working steps 1 and 2 along the line of the design, making the stitches smooth and even in size.

Basic hand stitches

There are some hand stitches that you will use time and again in many different situations when making sewing projects. In some cases it is much easier and quicker to hand stitch pieces together than to use a sewing machine, particularly if you are working with small pieces of fabric.

3 Running stitch

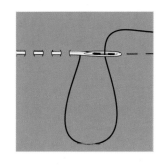

Used to join flat layers of fabric, or as a decoration. The stitches should be smaller and neater than tacking (basting) stitches. Take the needle in and out of the fabric several times, making a small stitch each time to create a row of evenly sized and spaced stitches. Pull the thread through gently until it is taut, but not too tight, then continue stitching as before.

4 Backstitch

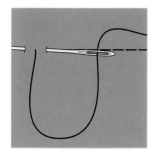

Used to join flat layers of fabric in a secure way, or as a decoration. From the front the stitches run end to end like machine stitching. Bring the needle through the fabric to the right side, then insert it a short distance behind where it came out and bring it up through the fabric the same distance ahead. Each subsequent stitch begins at the end of the previous stitch and the needle comes up again an equal distance ahead, so the stitches are the same size.

5 Slipstitch

Used to join two folded edges together, or a folded edge to a flat piece, so that the stitches are almost invisible. Bring the needle up through the folded edge of one side, take a tiny stitch through just one or 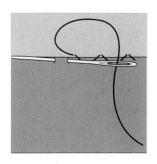 two threads in the opposite layer or fold, then insert the needle back into the fold of the first layer. Slide the needle along inside the fold a short way, then repeat the sequence.

6 Oversewing

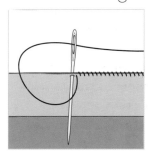

Another stitch used to join two folded edges. It is also known as whipstitch or overcasting. Insert the needle at a slight angle through the edges of both folds, picking up one or two threads on each edge. Pull the thread all the way through, then repeat the stitch. Whipstitch is usually worked from left to right, but there is no particular reason why it shouldn't be worked the other way if it feels more comfortable – as long as you are consistent.

Machine stitching

These basic machine stitches will be used throughout all sewing projects. Practise them on different weights and types of fabric.

7 Straight stitch

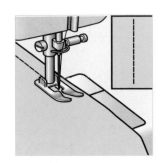

A row of simple, straight stitches used to join seams and to finish the edges of seams on knit fabrics. For most seams, the stitch length on the machine should be set to around 2 or 3. Topstitching is straight stitch worked on the right side of the fabric – sometimes in a contrasting colour thread – as a decorative touch or to hold a seam allowance or hem in place.

8 Backstitch

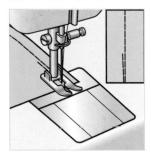

The reverse stitch on the sewing machine, used to reinforce the stitching at the beginning and end of a seam. Start off around 1cm (⅜in) from the beginning of the seam and reverse stitch back to the edge, then start stitching forward as normal. At the end, finish by reversing back along the stitching line for 1cm (⅜in).

9 Zigzag

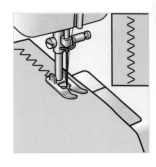

Most modern sewing machines have an automatic zigzag function. Zigzag stitching can be adjusted in the same way as straight stitching: the stitch width controls the width of the zigzag band and the stitch length controls how tightly together the stitches fall. Zigzag stitch is used to finish raw edges and to sew seams that need some give, such as on knit fabrics.

10 Plain seam

Pin the pieces of fabric right sides together. You can either mark the seamline or use the guides engraved on the sewing machine footplate to achieve an even seam allowance. For complex seams or slippery fabrics, it may be safer to tack the pieces together by hand before stitching. Sew the seam on the machine using a simple straight stitch with a short run of backstitching at each end to secure. Finally, remove the tacking threads and press the seam, either opened out flat or to one side, as instructed.

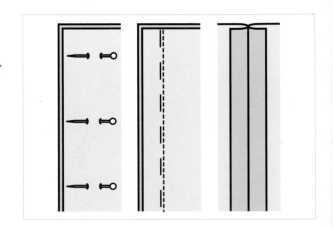

11 French seam

1 With wrong sides together, stitch the seam only 1cm (⅜in) from the edge. Trim the seam allowance to a scant 3mm (⅛in) and press it open.

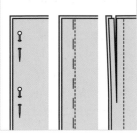

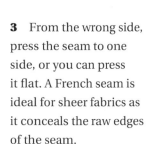

2 Fold the fabric right sides together along the stitching line you have just made. Pin and stitch a second seam on the seamline, enclosing the raw edges of the fabric.

Machine seams

The type of seam you choose for a project will be determined by the fabric, but also partly by the effect you want to achieve.

Finishing the raw edges of the seams 17 inside is just as important as the finishing touches to the outside. Finished seams not only give a garment a more professional look, they also prolong its life.

Always sew knitted fabrics with a ballpoint needle, as this will tend to slide between the fibres and not through them.

3 From the wrong side, press the seam to one side, or you can press it flat. A French seam is ideal for sheer fabrics as it conceals the raw edges of the seam.

12 Clipping curves

Inward or concave curves

Make little clips or snips in the seam allowance just up to, but not through, the line of stitching, so the seam will lie flat.

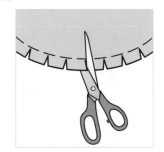

Outward or convex curves

Cut wedge-shaped notches from the seam allowance to eliminate excess fullness.

13 Clipping corners

Right angle

Using a pair of small, very sharp scissors, clip into the seam allowance, being careful not to cut through the stitching.

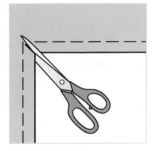

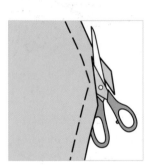

Obtuse angle

Using a pair of sharp scissors with a long blade, clip off the corner within the seam allowance, being careful not to cut through the stitching.

Acute angle

Using a pair of small, sharp scissors, clip into the point within the seam allowance, being careful not to cut through the stitching.

Clipping

Use sharp, pointed scissors to clip corners or notches – embroidery scissors are ideal.
Be very careful not to cut through the stitching – it is better to stop too short than to get too close. If you are sewing more than two layers of fabric together you can grade the seam by trimming the seam allowances back to different widths to prevent a bulky edge showing on the right side.

14 Making intersecting seams

1 Start by matching the seamlines on the two sections exactly, so they will run straight across the new seam at a right angle. To reduce the bulk of the extra thicknesses of fabric at the intersection, cut the seam allowances of the original seams into a point on both sides.

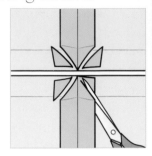

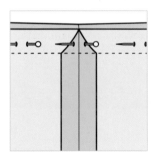

2 Pin on the seamlines to hold the sections in line, then pin or tack (baste) the rest of the new seam. Sew the new seam with a flat seam.

3 Press the new seam open. On the right side, the four seams should form a perfect cross shape with all the lines at right angles.

15 Lapped seam

This type of seam can be used on interfacing and wadding (batting) to reduce bulk, and also for fabrics that do not fray, such as leather. For interfacing and wadding (batting), simply lap the edges over one another

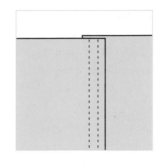

with the seamlines meeting in the centre, and stitch together along the seamline. For other materials such as leather, trim off the seam allowance along the edge of the upper piece, line up the newly cut edge with the seamline on the lower piece, and stitch together with a double row of straight stitch.

Turning the corner

To achieve a neat turn in a seam, stitch to the point at which you need to turn. Leaving the needle down in the fabric, lift the presser foot, swivel the work around to the new direction, lower the presser foot, then start stitching again. Trimming excess fabric from the corner **13** before you turn the item right side out will give a sharper point.

Knitted fabrics have more stretch than woven ones and seams need to have some give so the thread does not break. Use a zigzag stitch with a narrow stitch width and a medium length to sew the seam, or use an overlocker.

16 Pressing

Pressing is essential to achieve neat seams and a professional finish. You use only the tip of the iron and work quite lightly. Do not press over bulky areas, such as zips and pockets.

Flat seams

Remove any pins and tacking (basting) and, with the wrong side facing upward, open out the seam. Run the tip of the iron along the seam to press it flat.

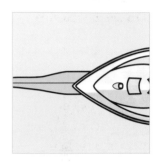

Finger pressing

Place the piece on a hard surface, wrong side upward, and run your finger along the seam to press flat. This technique is not suitable for any fabrics that will stretch or fray easily.

Clipped seams

Place the piece flat on the ironing board, wrong side upward, and the seam allowances lying together. Use the point of the iron to press back the top layer of the seam allowance.

Hems

Press hems from the fold towards the stitching, with wrong side uppermost, to avoid the edge showing on the right side.

Pressing chart

Heat	Fabric
Low	Acetate, shiny surfaces
Low to moderate	Blends, nylon, pile/nap, polyester, rayon, silk
Moderate	Acrylic, blends, wool
Moderate to high	Cotton
High	Linen

17 Seam finishes

Stitching or otherwise securing the raw edges of the seam allowance will give your seams a more professional look. It will also prolong the life of garments by protecting the edge of the seam during everyday wear. There are several different seam finishes you can consider.

Pinked seam

Stitch the seam, trim both the raw edges with pinking shears, then either press open or to one side. Use for most seams as long as the fabric does not fray.

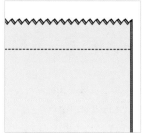

Double stitched

Stitch the seam, press, then make a second line of stitching right next to the first within the seam allowance. Use for seams subject to strain.

Zigzag stitched

Press open then zigzag stitch along each raw edge. If the seam is pressed to one side, zigzag both raw edges together. For most seams, and fabrics that may fray.

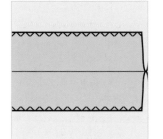

Turned and zigzagged

Turn under a very narrow hem along each raw edge and zigzag along the fold. Use for lightweight fabrics or fabrics that tend to fray.

Edge stitched

Turn under a very narrow hem along each raw edge and straight stitch **7** along the fold. Use for light- to medium-weight fabrics only.

Bias bound

Enclose the raw edge in a strip of bias binding and stitch through the binding close to the edge. If the seam must be pressed open, work both edges separately. If it is pressed closed both seams can be enclosed in the same strip of binding. Can be used for most seams, but particularly those on heavyweight fabrics that may fray.

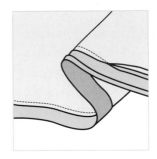

Hand oversewn

Turn under a very narrow hem along each raw edge and oversew **6** evenly by hand along the edge. Best used for heavier fabrics.

Hand hemmed

Turn under a very narrow double hem along each raw edge and slipstitch **5** . Good for very delicate fabrics.

Hems

The hems detailed here are suitable for both dressmaking and home furnishing projects. A hem can be hand or machine stitched; the choice depends on both the weight of the fabric and the style of the garment. Hemming is usually invisible, but may be used as a design element.

18 Simple machine-stitched hem

1 Measure, mark and tack (baste) two fold lines, one 5mm (¼in) from the raw edge and the other another 1cm (⅜in) away from the first. Turn the first fold under and press in place.

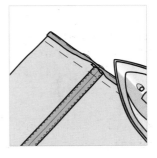

2 Turn under the second fold and press. Pin or tack (baste) the double layer of fabric into position, matching any seam positions.

3 On the wrong side of the fabric, stitch along next to the fold line, removing pins as you work. Remove any tacking (basting) and press the hem.

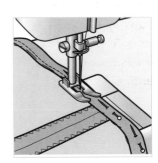

19 Simple hand-stitched hem

1 Measure the hem, then fold and press the bottom of the hem to mark it. Fold over the raw edge to the inside and press. Tack (baste) the fold lines to mark them and trim the raw edge to 5mm (¼in) from the second fold.

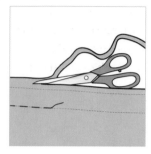

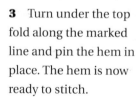

2 Fold up the hem along the line, matching the position of all of the seams as far as possible. You may need to ease the hem if the garment is flared. Tack (baste) around the hem through the centre of the fold.

3 Turn under the top fold along the marked line and pin the hem in place. The hem is now ready to stitch.

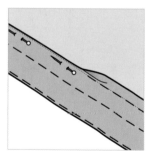

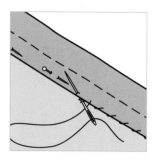

4 Lay the garment wrong side up on a flat surface. Slipstitch **5** along the fold, making sure stitches do not show on the right side. Remove pins and any tacking (basting) at the end.

20 Simple turn-up cuff

1 With the leg of the trousers (pants) wrong side out, fold and tack (baste) three parallel lines to mark the bottom edge of the turn-up, the top edge of the turn-up, and the hemline. Zigzag the raw edge, then turn

up the centre fold and press. Slipstitch to secure the zigzagged raw edge.

2 Turn the trouser (pant) leg right side out. Turn up the bottom fold to meet the line marking the top of the turn-up and press gently. Take a couple of small stitches at the side seams to secure the turn-up in position. Remove all the tacking (basting).

21 Hand-sewn hems

Try out some of the different types of hand-sewn hem to see which one will work best on your project.

Bound hem – made with either bias or straight binding. The binding is machine stitched to the raw edge of the marked hem, then turned up and pressed. It can either be hemmed or machine stitched in place.

Zigzagged hem – the raw edge is zigzag stitched and turned up and the hem held in place with herringbone stitch.

Edge-stitched hem – the raw edge is turned under and then edge stitched. The hem is turned up and pressed and stitched into position with ordinary hemming stitch.

Fusible hem – the hem is folded up and held in place with a strip of fusible hem tape. This can be suitable for lightweight fabrics and for emergency repairs, but the tape does tend to come loose after a while.

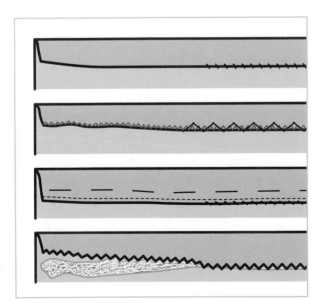

22 Single topstitched seam

This is a seam with an extra row of topstitching made on the right side. Although decorative, it can be functional; it can hold the seam allowance in place and prevent fraying. Press the seam allowance to one side.
Use either a matching or a contrasting thread and stitch with a small to medium-length stitch.

23 Double topstitched seam

A double topstitched seam has a row of topstitching on either side of the seam. Press the seam allowance flat on the wrong side, then topstitch down both sides on the right side, making sure that the two topstitched seams are an equal distance away from the seamline.

24 Gathering stitch

Gathering using a machine stitch gives a more even result, but if you don't have one you can sew a double line of running stitches 3 to gather the edge in the same way.

1 Set the stitch length at its longest and loosen the tension slightly. Stitch once just inside the seamline, then again in a parallel line a very short distance away.

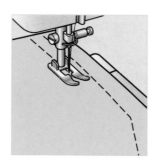

2 Tie the two top threads together on the right side of the fabric at one end, then tie the two bobbin threads together on the wrong side at the same end.

3 Pull both bobbin threads together at the untied end to gather up the fabric, easing the fabric along gently as you go. Adjust the gathers evenly along the required length, then fasten off the bobbin threads to secure.

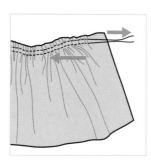

25 Making a casing for elastic

1 Measure the width of the waistband plus 5mm (¼in) and turn over the waist edge of the garment to the inside. Turn under the raw edge by 5mm (¼in). Topstitch along the bottom edge to create a casing, leaving a gap unstitched. Thread the waist elastic through the gap.

2 Pull the two ends of the elastic clear of the fabric and pin together. Make sure the strip of elastic is not twisted along its length, then stitch the two ends together firmly, either by slipstitching along the double layer edges, or by machine stitching a square on the overlapping section. Close the gap in the edge by topstitching across it to match the original topstitching.

3 This technique can also be used for an elasticated cuff or hem. On translucent fabrics, however, the casing would show through. You could get the same effect by stitching rows of shirring elastic on the wrong side.

26 Gathered waistband with separate elasticized casing

1 Stitch the short ends of the waistband casing together, leaving a gap in the seam on one side, to thread the elastic through in step 4. Press the centre fold down the length of the waistband casing strip, wrong sides together. Stitch the long edges together.

4 Thread the elastic through the vertical gap in the waistband seam. Overlap the two ends of elastic and stitch together to secure. Slide the remaining elastic inside the opening, then stitch it closed.

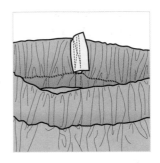

2 Run a double line of gathering threads around the waistline of the garment, within the seamline. Pull up the threads to gather the fabric evenly around the waist, to the length of the waistband.

5 For a drawstring instead of elastic, make sure the vertical gap in the casing seam falls to the inside when stitching the casing to the garment. This ensures that it falls on the outside when the waistband is finished. Thread the drawstring and tie in a bow.

3 Pin then stitch the waistband casing to the waistline of the garment with right sides together, matching notches and seams and easing the gathers evenly. The vertical gap to insert the elastic should fall on the side of the casing facing you at this stage.

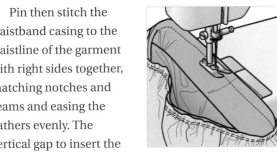

Binding and borders

Making your own edgings gives you a much greater choice of fabric as well as the option of coordinating with other items. Binding is a narrow band of fabric that encloses a raw edge. Borders are wider and may either enclose the edge or be added to it. Both can be made in matching or contrasting fabrics, but try to use fabric that is the same weight as the main fabric for the best result.

27 Making bias binding

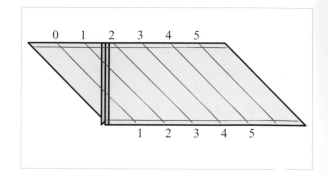

1 Make sure the end of the length is straight on the grain and then fold it down to line up with the selvedge at one side.

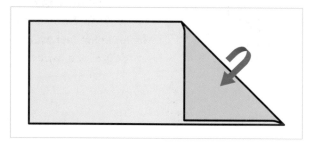

2 Cut along the fold line, then take the triangle of fabric you have just removed and stitch it to the other end of the piece to make the parallelogram shape shown left.

3 Mark a series of lines parallel with the diagonal edge, set apart by twice the width of the binding. Number the bands 1, 2, 3, etc. down the bottom edge with an air-erasable marker. On the top edge, mark the lines as shown, which will offset the numbers.

4 With right sides together, bring the edges round and match the numbers so 1 lines up with 1, 2 with 2, and so on. The zero and the last number will not match with anything. Stitch the seam with a 1cm (⅜in) seam allowance, to create a tube of fabric. Press the seam open.

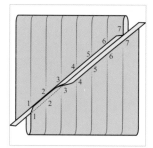

5 Cut along the marked line, which now runs around the tube in a continuous spiral. Fold both edges of the strip towards the middle and press in position, being careful not to stretch the bias binding as you work. A bias binding maker will make this process easier.

Joining bias strips

1   If you need to join two strips of bias binding, do it before you fold the edges over. Pin the strips right sides together (they will form an L-shape). Stitch together, leaving a 2.5cm (1in) seam allowance.

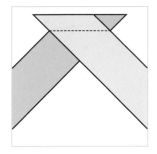

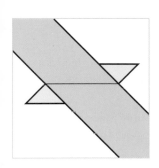

2   Press the seam open. Remember that if the bias strip has a pattern, you should try to match it on the seamline, not on the cut edges. Trim off the protruding points, and fold over the edges as in step 5, below left.

28 Binding a straight edge

1   Open out the fold along one edge of the bias binding and place it right sides together on the edge to be bound, with raw edges matching. Pin in place, being careful not to stretch either edge.

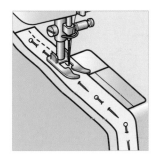

2   Straight stitch 7 along the fold line of the bias binding, removing the pins as you work.

3   Fold the binding around the raw edges to the wrong side. If you don't want the binding to show, fold on the stitching line. If you want a narrow border of binding, fold on the centre line of the binding.

4   Stitch along the folded edge on the wrong side, either slipstitching 5 if you don't want the stitches to show or with the machine.

Stitching by hand

Start with a length of thread about 60cm (24in) long – if it is any longer it may tangle after being pulled through the fabric a few times. Always buy good-quality thread: cheap thread breaks easily when you are working or after the item is completed.

29 Blanket stitch

Although it can be used decoratively, blanket stitch is also used to finish raw edges. Buttonhole stitch is very similar, but the uprights are worked right next to one another.

1 Come up through the fabric at A, go down at B and up again at C immediately to the right of A. Loop the thread under the point of the needle from left to right. Pull the thread through.

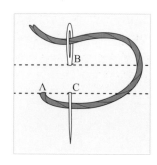

2 Go down into the fabric at D a short way to the right of B, and up at E. Loop the thread under the point of the needle again and then pull the thread through.

3 Continue working in this way along the line or edge, keeping the stitches evenly sized and spaced.

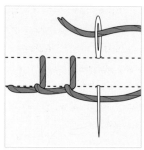

30 Chain stitch and lazy daisy stitch

A decorative looped stitch that can be used to make a chain line, or worked in a circle to make a flower.

1 Come up through the fabric at A, then go down into it again slightly to the left of A and come up to the surface again at B. Loop the thread under the point of the needle from right to left.

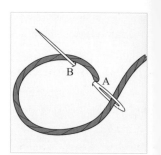

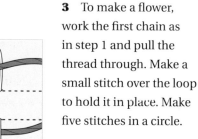

2 Pull the thread through. Start the next chain by going down into the fabric again slightly to the left of B, inside the first loop, and then up at C. Loop the thread around the point again.

3 To make a flower, work the first chain as in step 1 and pull the thread through. Make a small stitch over the loop to hold it in place. Make five stitches in a circle.

31 Satin stitch

Sometimes known as damask stitch, this is one of the basic embroidery stitches, used as a filling stitch and as the basis for a wide variety of more complex stitches. For best results, stretch the fabric on a hoop or frame to keep it taut as you work.

1 Come up through the fabric at A, then go down into it again at B on the other side of the shape to be filled. Come up again at C, right next to A.

2 From C go down into the fabric again at D on the other side of the shape to be filled. Come up again at E, right next to C.

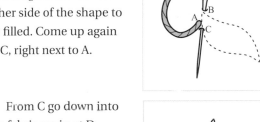

3 Continue in this way to fill in the shape completely with a series of straight stitches worked very closely together to create a smooth surface with no fabric showing beneath.

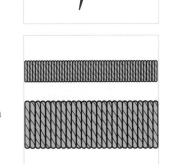

4 Satin stitch can also be worked in straight rows to create a decorative border, which can be narrow or wider.

32 French knot

A versatile stitch that creates a small bead on the surface of the fabric. It can be used to add texture or create details.

1 Come up through the fabric at A and wrap the thread around the needle once in an anticlockwise direction.

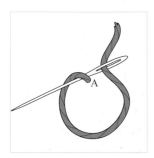

2 Keeping the needle away from the fabric, wrap the thread around the needle a second time in the same way.

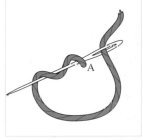

3 Push the wraps together, and slide them to the end of the needle. Take the needle down near where it came out of the fabric, pulling the thread through to create a knot.

33 Cross stitch

This stitch has been used for centuries in all kinds of ways, in many different scales and with several variations.

1   To make one cross stitch, come up through the fabric at A, go down into it again at B, up at C and down again at D. Fasten off on the reverse, or come up through the fabric again to work the next stitch.

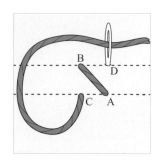

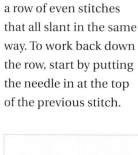

2   To make a row of cross stitches, first work a row of even stitches that all slant in the same way. To work back down the row, start by putting the needle in at the top of the previous stitch.

3   Work diagonal stitches back down the row, slanting the other way, to form a line of even crosses.

34 Fused appliqué

Fusible webbing has made appliqué much quicker and easier, and is particularly good for working with complicated shapes.

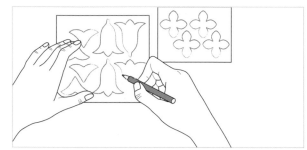

1   Trace all the appliqué shapes on to the paper backing of the fusible webbing – the shapes can be drawn quite close together to save on materials.

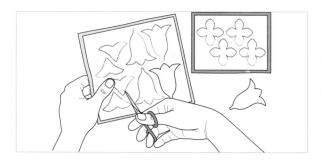

2   Cut off the areas of fusible webbing with the motifs, and iron them on to the reverse side of the fabrics you will be using for the appliqué, following the instructions on the fusible webbing packet.

3 On the background
fabric, mark the centre
point of where the motif
will be positioned,
or place the pattern
underneath to act as a
position guide.

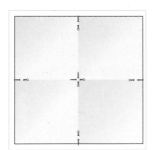

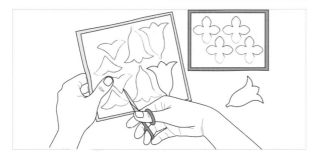

4 Peel the backing paper off the appliqué motifs
and carefully place the first pieces on the background
fabric. Iron into position, again following the
instructions on the fusible webbing packet.

5 Add the remaining pieces and iron into place.
To finish, hand embroider or satin stitch by machine
around the edges.

Working in reverse

Remember that if you are working on the back
of the fabric, the motif will be reversed when it is
right side up. With most shapes this may not be a
problem, but if you are using letters or numbers as
part of the design trace them in reverse in step 1.

When tracing the shapes on to the backing of the
fusible webbing, group pieces in the same colour
and cut them out in one block to iron to the
fabric. This means you only have to cut carefully
around each shape once.

35 Inserted trim

1 Cut the main piece as required. Cut four strips of lace the length of the edges of the main piece, plus twice the width of the lace. Cut four border strips twice the required border depth and the length of the very outside edge of the item.

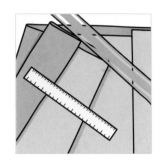

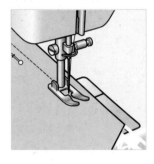

2 Pin and stitch a length of lace to one edge of the main piece, right sides together, leaving the ends unstitched for the moment. Work one side at a time, centring the strip of lace on the edge each time.

3 Turn the lace out and press flat. Make a neat mitre (see tip box) in the corner of each strip of lace, or join the end of each strip by overlapping the next.

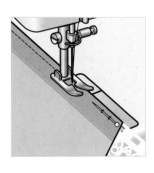

4 With right sides together, pin the border strips to the outside edge of the lace all round, leaving overlaps on all the corners as you did on the lace.

5 Press under the raw edge of a border strip and fold it back to cover the raw edge of the lace on the reverse. Pin in place. At the corner, fold under the short end of the border level with the outer edge of the lace.

Press under the short edge of the next border level with the outer edge of the first, then press under the long raw edge and fold back to cover the edge of the lace as before.

7 Topstitch around all sides of the item along the fold at the lace edge, making a neat square at each of the corners, as shown here. The overlap method works best for most lace designs, but for some a mitred join will be better.

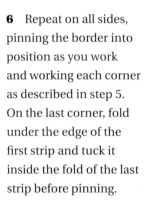

6 Repeat on all sides, pinning the border into position as you work and working each corner as described in step 5. On the last corner, fold under the edge of the first strip and tuck it inside the fold of the last strip before pinning.

Making a mitre on an insert strip

To mitre the lace strips, first centre the design on each side of the cloth. Cut the strips of lace so they overlap by at least the width of the strip at each corner. Add the strips as described in step 2 opposite. At the corner, fold the cloth diagonally through the centre of the corner, with right sides together. Stitch the ends of the lace together at the corner along a line that is a continuation of the diagonal fold you just made. When the fold is opened out, the lace strips will be neatly mitred at each corner.

36 Mitred corner

1 At the corner turn up the seam allowances and press along the seamline in both directions. Open the seam flat and turn over the corner triangle so the diagonal line runs through the intersection of the pressed lines. Press the diagonal line to make a crease.

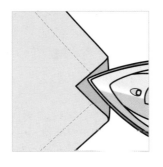

4 Turn the corners right side out. Turn under the raw edges on each side of the hem and pin in place. Stitch the hem to secure.

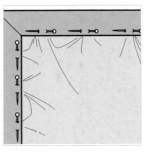

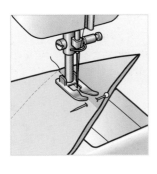

2 Open the corner and fold the fabric through the corner diagonally, with right sides together so the raw edges and hemline creases meet. Pin and then stitch along the diagonal creased line made in step 1.

5 The finished item should have neat corners on both sides. This method is not only used on home furnishings, such as tablecloths and placemats, but is also useful for jacket fronts and skirt slits.

3 Trim off the excess triangular piece of seam allowance from the corner and press the seam open. Repeat on all corners of the piece that is to be mitred.

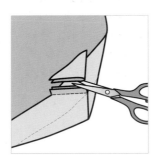

Piping and cording

Piping is a strip of flat, folded fabric inserted into a seam for decoration, while cording is piping with a cord inside the fold, giving it a more rounded appearance. Piping gives a soft, rounded finish, whereas cording is firmer and gives a more sculpted look. Cord for piping comes in a range of thicknesses, and both cording and piping can be made with matching or contrasting fabrics and colours.

37 Piping and cording

1 For piping, make a strip of bias binding twice the width you want the piping to be, plus 3cm (1¼in) for the seam allowances. For cording, it should be three times the width of the cord, plus the seam allowances.

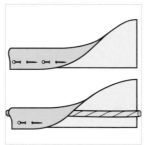

3 On the seam that is to be piped or corded, place the fabrics right sides together with the piping or cording in between and all raw edges aligned. Pin or tack (baste) together.

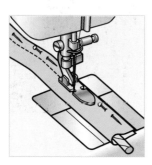

2 Fold the strip in half, wrong sides together and raw edges aligned. For cording, insert the cord into the fold and stitch along the strip close to the cord using a zip foot on your machine.

4 Stitch along the seamline, being careful not to catch the cord in the seam as you work. Use a zip foot on your machine for cording; for piping you can just use the ordinary foot.

38 Using purchased cord

1 Wrap one end of the cord with masking tape. Stitch the cord to the edge of the item by hand, making a stitch through the cord and then through the fabric. At the end, wrap tape around the other end of the cord, allowing the two ends to overlap.

2 Unpick around 2.5cm (1in) of the seam next to the overlapped cord. Remove the tape from the cord and slip the ends into the gap in the seam, overlapping them slightly. Slipstitch the seam closed, securing the cord at the same time.

39 Frilled edge

1 Cut a frill strip to the desired width plus seam allowances and twice the length of the edge to have the frill. Stitch a narrow double hem along one edge of the frill and run a double line of gathering stitches **24** along the other edge.

2 Pin the frill with right sides together around the edge, matching raw edges and with the frill turned to the inside. Machine tack (baste) the frill all around the edge.

3 Lay the front piece right side up and align the back piece or facing over it, right side down and matching all raw edges. Pin and stitch along the edges, then zigzag stitch to finish off all raw edges. Remove the pins and turn the item right side out.

Pockets

The most important thing about pockets is that they should be strong enough to withstand normal wear and tear. They are usually made of the same material as the garment, but may be lined with a lighter fabric to lessen bulk. Patch pockets are added to the outside face of a garment and may be lined or unlined. Alternatively, pockets can be attached to the waist and side seams and sit inside the garment. On jackets and some tailored garments the pocket is concealed behind the front, and only a welt band trimming the opening can be seen on the outer surface.

40 Basic patch pocket

1 Mark the pocket on the garment using an erasable marking method, and transfer markings to the wrong side of the pocket piece. Tack (baste) the seamline of the pocket and zigzag **9** the top raw edge.

2 Fold over the top edge of the pocket. Make sure the right sides are together and any positioning marks match. Pin in place.

3 Stitch across the ends of the folded section from the top fold to the zigzag stitching only. Clip across the top corners.

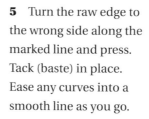

4 Turn the top section right side out and ease the corners to a sharp point – you can use a pin to gently ease them out but be careful not to pull a thread loose.

5 Turn the raw edge to the wrong side along the marked line and press. Tack (baste) in place. Ease any curves into a smooth line as you go.

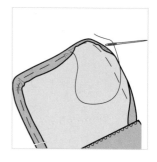

6 The finished patch pocket is now ready to be applied to the garment.

7 Pin the pocket on the garment, following the positioning marks. Place the pins at right angles away from the seam so you can stitch without having to remove them.

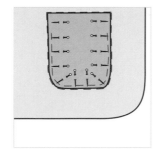

8 Check you are happy with the pocket position, as it can easily be altered at this stage. If so, stitch in place with a double line of stitching.

41 Sewing buttons

1 There are two basic types of button. The sew-through button has several holes – usually two or four, but sometimes three – that run right through the button. The shank button has a plain or decorative front surface and a loop or shank on the back.

3 To make a thread shank for a sew-through button, place a matchstick or toothpick on top of the button and sew over it. Remove the stick, lift the button, and wind the thread around the extra length of thread between the button and the garment. Bring the needle to the underside of the garment and fasten with several small stitches.

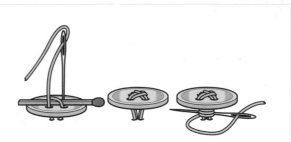

2 Sew-through buttons must be stitched through the holes provided so the stitching thread will show. They may require a thread shank on the back to hold them away from the surface of the fabric to allow for the thickness of the buttonhole fabric layer. The shank button is sewn on through the shank at the back so the stitching thread is not visible and the shank also holds the button above the fabric surface.

42 Machine-sewn buttonhole

1 Mark the centre position and length of the buttonhole by tacking (basting) guidelines on the button band, using the button as a guide.

4 Repeat steps 2 and 3 to work the other side and end of the buttonhole. Set the stitch width at 0 to make a few stitches to secure the end of the thread.

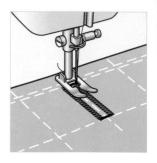

2 Run a line of straight stitching on each side of the line of the buttonhole opening. Set the machine to medium-width zigzag and stitch a row of tight satin stitch along one edge.

5 Pull any loose ends through to the wrong side and trim close to the fabric. Using a seam ripper or a very sharp pair of scissors, slit the buttonhole open down the centre line.

3 Raise the foot and turn the garment 180 degrees, then make a few long stitches across the full buttonhole width to reinforce the end.

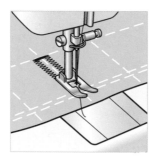

Automatic buttonholes

Some more modern machines will stitch the entire buttonhole automatically, using a special foot that holds the button as a reference for sizing the buttonhole. If you have this type of machine, follow the instructions in the manual to mark the buttonhole and set up the machine.

43 Centre zip

1 Mark the zip position on the seam, using the zip as a guide. Stitch the seam to the bottom mark, leaving enough room at the top for a facing seam. Zigzag the raw edges.

2 Place the closed zip over the seam on the wrong side and pin in place. Tack (baste) along both sides to hold it firmly in position while you work. Turn the garment to the right side.

3 Using a zip foot on the machine, start at the top and stitch down one side, across the bottom, and up to the top again to secure the zip in place. Move the zip slider if necessary to keep the seam straight, and keep the bottom corners nice and square.

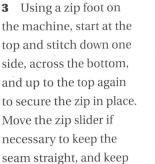

4 Add the facing or the waistband piece to the garment in the normal way and slipstitch the ends to the zip tape. Make sure that no stitches or facings are likely to catch in the zip teeth in use. Remove any tacking (basting) and add any other fasteners required at the top edge.

44 Lapped zip

1   Stitch the seam to the bottom of the zip and zigzag the raw edges of the seam allowance. Open the zip and pin and tack (baste) it to one side of the seam allowance, which will become the underlap.

Working from the wrong side, stitch this seam with the zip foot on the machine. Strengthen the raw edge of the overlap seam with seam tape.

2   Fold the overlap edge to the wrong side of the garment. Pin and tack (baste) the zip into position along both sides of the zip tape, then close the zip.

3   Again using the zip foot on the machine, stitch the closed zip in place on the overlap side and across the bottom. Remove the tacking (basting). Check to make sure that the zip slides easily when it is opened and closed, and that it is fully hidden in the seam.

45 Fly-front zip

1   Cut out and prepare the garment pieces. Finish all raw edges with zigzag stitch and tack (baste) all the zip markings as shown on the pattern.

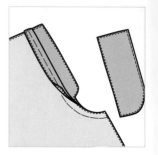

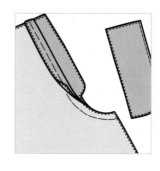

2   Fold the fly piece in half lengthwise, wrong sides together, and topstitch 3mm (1/8in) from the fold. Zigzag the other edges together. Stitch the curved garment seam, then fold the underlap to the wrong side and tack (baste) along the fold.

3   Open the zip and align the teeth with the underlap fold. Pin, tack (baste) and stitch the zip on the underlap near the teeth, leaving room for the slider to move up and down. Close the zip, fold the overlap along the tacked (basted) line, and tack (baste) through all layers of the overlap.

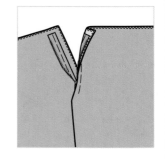

4 Pin the fly piece over the closed zip, making sure that the curved edges match. Tack (baste) in position along the seamline.

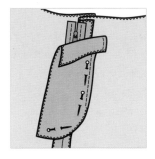

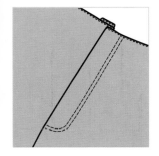

5 Working on the right side, work a double row of topstitching to reinforce the finished fly, following the curved line of the tacking (basting) on the fly piece.

Simple Stitching

This section has a collection of easy projects with little shaping and no complex seaming to get you started. You only need basic stitching techniques – although the final result will still look great! As you learn further stitching skills, you will find these projects are also ideal as the basis for extra embellishments.

Apron

This would make a fantastic present for someone who loves to cook, and is ideal for those who prefer a half apron with a useful pocket at the front. It's a very quick project to make and takes very little fabric – choose material that might match the recipient's kitchen or their favourite colours. Here we have used some gorgeous polka-dotted fabric in a duck egg blue.

Size
One size fits all

You will need
125cm (50in) length of 112cm (45in) wide fabric
Tape measure
Fabric scissors
Pins
Sewing needle
Thread to match fabric
Iron

1 For the apron, cut one piece 78cm (30¾in) wide × 46cm (18in) long. For the straps, cut two pieces each 80cm (31½in) long × 8cm (3¼in) wide to tie in a bow at the back.

2 On one long edge of the main apron, turn over the raw edge once by approx 1cm (⅜in), then turn over again by approx 2cm (¾in) to make a double hem. Pin, stitch **7** and press **16** . Repeat this step on the other long edge.

3 Double hem **18** the two remaining sides using the same method but making the hem narrower, approx 1cm (⅜in) wide.

4 For the patch pocket **40** , cut a piece of fabric 28cm (11in) wide × 21cm (8¼in) long. Fold over one long edge by 5mm (¼in) and then by 1cm (⅜in) to make a double hem at the top of the pocket. Pin and stitch across. On the other three sides, fold under the edges once by 2cm (¾in). Press, pin and tack (baste) **2** the folds in place.

5 Place the pocket onto the front of the apron in the centre, with the bottom edge 8cm (3¼in) up from the bottom. Pin in place. Sew around the three sides, leaving the top open. Measure the pocket and place a marker pin at the top, middle and bottom down the centre line. Sew a straight line from top to bottom of the pocket to divide it into two sections. Remove the tacking (basting).

6 Fold one piece of strap fabric in half lengthways and press. Open it out flat and fold both long raw edges to the centre fold line. Press.

7 Fold the strap in half again, press, pin and then sew down one long side, just in from the open edge.

8 At one end, fold the raw edges of the strap inside and pin. Sew in place. Repeat on the other strap.

9 Fold in the other end of the strap in the same way and slipstitch **5** this end of the strap firmly in place at one end of the apron waistband. Repeat for the other strap.

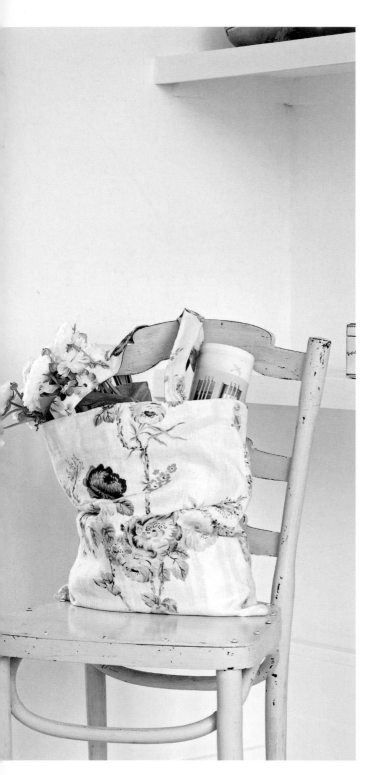

Shopper

This bag is not only a fantastic shopping bag, but can also be used as a book bag for children, a vegetable bag, a swimming bag, a laundry bag – anything. It's also reversible, so if you get bored with one design then simply turn it inside out and use the other side. Within just an hour or two you will have transformed a simple piece of fabric into something inspiring. Once you have made one, you'll realize just how easy it is and you'll be making more bags for all your friends and family.

Size
36cm (14¼in) wide and 39.5cm (16in) long

You will need
75cm (30in) of 90cm (36in) wide main fabric
75cm (30in) of 90cm (36in) wide contrast lining fabric
Tape measure
Fabric scissors
Pins
Sewing needle
Thread to match fabric
Iron

Tip
Press all the seams open after sewing.

1 Measure and cut two 39 × 46cm (15¾ × 17¼in) pieces in both the main fabric and the lining fabric.

2 Using the main fabric, pin the back and front pieces together with right sides facing. Sew a plain seam **10** down two sides and across the bottom with a 1.5cm (⅝in) seam allowance. Remove the pins.

3 Repeat step 2 with the two pieces of lining fabric.

4 Clip diagonally **13** across the two bottom corners of both lining and main fabric, being very careful not to cut into the stitching.

5 Press **16** all the seams open on the main fabric and lining by pressing the seam down one side first, then turning the bag over and pressing down the other side of the seam.

6 Turn the main fabric bag right side out, making sure the corners are neat and square.

7 Put your hand inside the lining fabric bag and slip the main fabric bag over the top, smoothing the creases and easing the two layers together. Make sure that the lining fabric is thoroughly inside the main bag and that the seams are aligned.

8 Measure 33cm (13in) from the bottom of the bag and place a marker pin in three places along the top edge, on each side of the bag.

9 Turn under the main fabric at the marker points, press and then take out the marker pins. Pin the folded-over top in place ready for sewing.

10 Fold the lining fabric inside to meet the fold along the top of the main fabric bag, making sure that the lining and the main fabric are at exactly the same height. Press the fold in place.

14 Slide the ends of one of the straps between the lining and the main fabric on one side of the bag. Each end of the strap should be positioned 8cm (3¼in) from the side seam of the bag. Pin in place.

15 Turn the bag over and insert the other strap in the same way, making sure it is exactly the same distance from the side seams as the strap on the other side. Pin so that both bag handles are an equal length.

11 Cut two strips 58 × 6cm (23 × 2½in) from both the lining fabric and the main fabric. On one of the main fabric strips, fold over by a quarter of the width down the entire length of the strip. Press in place, then repeat on the other side of the strip.

12 Repeat with the other main fabric strip and both lining fabric strips.

16 Sew around the top edge of the bag, catching the ends of the straps as you sew. Use the edge of the machine foot as your width marker. Press.

17 Sew a small hand stitch in the bottom corners of the bag, so that when you reverse or wash it, the two fabric layers will stay together.

13 Put one lining and one main fabric strip together with folded edges aligned and all raw edges to the inside. Pin in place. Topstitch **7** down each edge of the strap as near to the edge as possible. Repeat to make the other strap.

Basic Cushion

Simple square cushions (throw pillows) are very quick and easy to make and are great to add more colour or interest to plain seating – or to make a hard seat more comfortable. If you have left-over fabric from curtains or other soft furnishings you can quickly run up a few matching cushions to coordinate with your colour scheme.

Size
To fit a 40cm (16in) square cushion (throw pillow)

You will need
50cm (20in) of 112cm (45in) wide plain fabric
Tape measure
Fabric scissors
Sewing machine or sewing needle
Thread to match fabric
Fusible webbing
Motif – we used the letter A
Pencil
30cm (12in) square of contrast appliqué fabric
Iron
Stranded embroidery thread (floss) in a
    contrasting colour
Embroidery needle
40cm (16in) square cushion pad (pillow form)

1 Measure and cut the following pieces from the plain fabric: one 43cm (17¼in) square, one rectangle 27 × 43cm (10½ × 17¼in) and one rectangle 33 × 43cm (13 × 17¼in). Zigzag **9** around all the raw edges to prevent the pieces from fraying.

2 Find a suitable letter or motif to use as a template and copy it onto the paper side of the fusible webbing and then fuse **34** it onto the wrong side of the contrast appliqué fabric.

3 Cut out the fused shape and peel off the backing paper. Position the shape in the centre of the square of plain fabric, right side up. Fuse the shape to the square using the iron as before.

4 Using three strands of the embroidery thread (floss), hand embroider around the shape in small running stitches **3** , using the photograph as a guide. Add further stitched details if you wish.

5 Make a 5cm (2in) double hem along one long edge of each rectangle piece. Either machine stitch **18** or hand stitch **19** each hem in place.

6 With right sides up, pin the two rectangles with the hems overlapping to make a 43cm (17¼in) square. With right sides together, pin this square to the appliquéd front cover. Machine stitch **10** around all four edges with a 1.5cm (⅝ in) seam allowance.

7 Clip across the corners **13** . Turn the cover right side out through the hole in the back and press **16** . Insert the cushion pad (pillow form) through the envelope back to finish.

Shoulder Bag

This bag almost qualifies as a rucksack, because you can cram so much in it; however, the long shoulder strap is worn across the body and over one shoulder, distributing the weight and leaving you with your hands free. There is a handy outer pocket for items that you need instant access to. The bag and strap sections are cut in a single piece for ease of construction. Make this bag now – it's so useful that you'll wonder how you ever managed without it!

Size

Approx 50cm (20in) wide × 42cm (17in) high, excluding straps

You will need

2.5m (2⅝yd) × 112cm (44in) of thick cotton or linen
Tape measure
Fabric scissors
Pins
Tailor's chalk or erasable fabric marker
Sewing machine (optional)
Sewing needle
Thread to match fabric
Iron
3.5m (3¾yd) of 1.5cm (⅝in) wide bias binding

1   Cut out the fabric according to the pattern pieces on page 120. Pin the pocket with wrong sides together. Tack (baste) **2** and then stitch around the curved edge with a 1cm (⅜in) seam. Turn right side out and press **16** .

2   Apply bias binding **28** to the raw edge of the top of the pocket, folding in the ends to neaten. Place the pocket on the front bag piece and pin in position. Tack (baste), then topstitch **7** close to the edge around three sides, leaving the top open.

3   To make the outside of the bag, place one pair of front and back bag pieces with right sides together, then pin, tack (baste) and sew with a 1cm (⅜in) seam **10** . Sew right around the outer edge of the bag and strap, leaving the hole in the centre open. Do the same with the lining. Press. Turn the bag right side out; leave the lining wrong side out.

4   Pin bias binding around the raw edges of the straps and opening edges of the bag.

5   Make a tuck in the binding as you feed it around the corners.

6   Slip the lining inside the bag, so the wrong side of the lining faces the wrong side of the bag, the seams of the outer edge of bag/strap and lining/strap match, and the raw edges are even. Fold the binding over to enclose the raw edges of both the bag and lining and slipstitch **5** in place on the inside.

Lace Bow Top

I love designing extremely simple pieces that you can dress up as the mood takes you, and this dainty floral summer blouse was inspired by loose-fitting Japanese garment styles. It is the perfect shape for keeping cool on the warmest of days, and is a cinch to make. It has a boat neckline and a pretty lace tie at the waist – use a single piece of lace or several in different widths. Wear the blouse with a corsage for extra glamour.

Size

To fit size Small, Medium, Large (see page 121)

You will need

1.25m (1⅜ yd) of 112cm (45in) lightweight cotton, such as lawn or voile (sprigged cotton)
Tape measure
Fabric scissors
Tailor's chalk or erasable fabric marker
Pins
Sewing machine
Matching thread
Sewing needle
2.25m (2½yd) of 9–10cm (3½–4in) wide lace trim
6.5m (7yd) of 1cm (⅜in) lace trim (optional)

1   Cut out the fabric for the back and front of the blouse according to the pattern on page 121. Join the sides and shoulders with a French seam **11**.

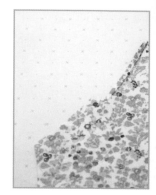

2   Finish the neck and armhole edges with a narrow hem – fold about 5mm (¼in) to the inside, then fold over the same amount again. Pin and tack (baste) **2**, then machine in place.

3   Hem the bottom of the blouse by folding 1cm (⅜in) to the inside, then folding over the same amount again. Pin and tack (baste), then machine the hem **18** in place.

4   Place the centre of the wide piece of lace on the side seam in a suitable position on the outside of the blouse. Pin, tack (baste) and machine stitch **7** down the centre of the side seam.

5   If you wish to add the narrow lace as well, cut it into three equal pieces and arrange the centres over the stitching on the wide lace. Stitch in place. Finish the ends of the lace ties if desired. For cotton lace, just fold over the end and oversew **6**. For synthetic lace, apply binding to the end and then fold over and hem.

Patchwork Blanket

If you have a love for fabrics and can't stop yourself from buying pieces of old material, or if you have clothes that you simply can't throw away, patchwork is perfect for you – particularly in light of current trends for being thrifty and recycling. Start making a collection of 15cm (6in) squares – you will need 108 squares for a good size blanket, but make it bigger if you need it for a bed or a large sofa.

Size
110 × 146cm (44 × 57in)

You will need
108 × 15cm (6in) squares of cotton fabric in various colours and prints
Iron
15cm (6in) patchwork template square
Tape measure
Fabric scissors
Sewing needle
Thread to match the fabric
1.5m (1¾yd) of 115cm (46in) wide fleece
6m (6½yd) of 7.5cm (3in) wide ribbon or a strip of fabric this size

1   Press 16 each piece of fabric before cutting out 108 assorted pieces each 15cm (6in) square, using the patchwork template.

2   Lay out the squares on the floor or on a large table and move them around to make sure you haven't got two squares the same next to each other.

3   Take two squares and, with right sides facing, sew them together with a 5mm (¼in) seam 10. Continue joining the squares together in rows, until you have nine rows of nine squares. Press all the seams open.

4   Pin and sew the strips together, matching seam to seam. Press all seams flat.

5   Place the fleece fabric right side down on a flat surface and push out any creases. Lay the patchwork on top of the fleece, right side up, and pin the two layers together. Cut the fleece to the same size as the blanket. Pin and sew 7 the fleece to the patchwork as close to the edges as possible.

6   Using a hand-sewing needle and thread, take a couple of backstitches 4 right through the fleece and the patchwork top in each corner of the squares. Pull the thread through several times and secure with a knot. This holds the fleece and the patchwork aligned with each other.

7   Fold the ribbon or strip of fabric in half lengthways. With the patchwork side of the blanket facing, pin the binding 28 to the blanket with raw edges aligned. Work in sequence by first pinning along one side, then cutting the ribbon to length leaving a 3cm (1¼in) overlap. Repeat on the opposite side. Sew along both lengths close to the edge. Remove any remaining pins.

8   Fold the binding over the raw edge of the blanket and pin on the fleece side. Slipstitch 5 both strips of binding to the fleece.

9   Repeat on the remaining two sides of the blanket. Trim and fold the corners of the edging neatly, then hand sew in place.

Shaping and Fastening

In this section we move on to making some simple toys, as well as some easy items of clothing with gathering and fastenings. These projects will help you try out some additional seams and simple embroidery, as well as practise inserting a zip.

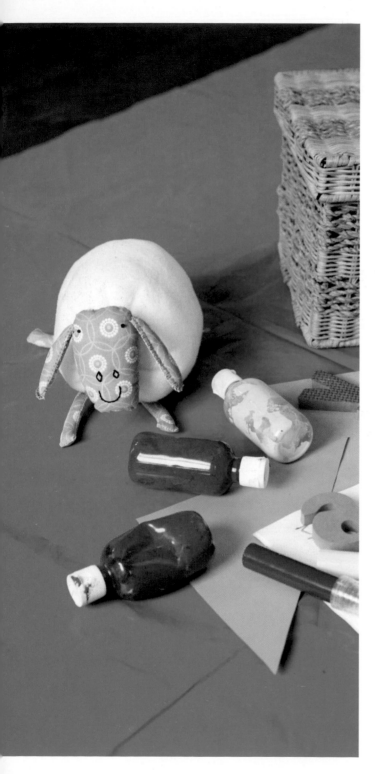

Olivia the Sheep

Olivia is a lively sheep and can't wait to get up to mischief with her new owner! She is bound to be a hit: her soft, round body is very cuddly and her little legs give her a slightly comic appearance.

Size
Approx 40cm (15¾in) long

You will need
41 × 22cm (16 × 8½in) of white or cream fleece
Pins
Sewing machine
Sewing thread to match fabric
Toy stuffing
Scraps of pale patterned cotton fabric
Stranded embroidery thread (floss) in yellow and black
Embroidery needle

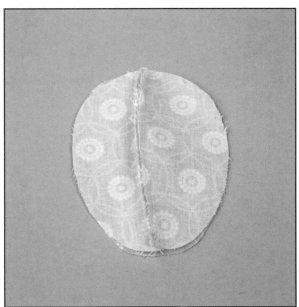

1   To make the sheep's body, fold the rectangle of fleece in half widthways, with right sides together, so the two shorter sides meet. Pin and tack (baste) **2** along the short edge. Machine stitch with a 1.5cm (⅝in) seam **10**, leaving a gap in the middle for turning.

2   Run a gathering stitch **24** by hand or machine all the way around one of the ends, 5mm (¼in) away from the edge, and pull it up tightly. Sew over and over the end so that no hole remains, flattening the sticking-out bit as you do so. Repeat at the other end of the body.

3   Turn the body right side out and stuff quite firmly, then pin or tack (baste) the gap closed.

4   Use the templates on page 125 to cut out the pieces for the head, ears, legs and tail. Place the two pieces for the back of the head with right sides together. Pin, tack (baste) and machine stitch with a 5mm (¼in) seam. Pin the front and back of the head with right sides together, then tack (baste). Machine stitch around the edge with a 5mm (¼in) seam, leaving a gap for turning. Turn right side out and stuff.

5   Place two pieces for each ear with wrong sides together. Pin and tack (baste). Embroider around the edge of each ear with three strands of yellow embroidery thread (floss), using blanket stitch **29** and leaving the top of the ear open.

6   Stuff the ears lightly. Sew the ears to the head using three strands of yellow embroidery thread (floss) – work blanket stitch along the top of the ear, catching the ear to the head at the same time.

7 Embroider the facial features using six strands of black embroidery thread (floss). For the eyes, work French knots **32** with three loops. Backstitch **4** the mouth and nose using the photo as a guide.

8 To close the head, turn in 5mm (¼in) and slipstitch the edges together. Slipstitch **5** the head to the body with a double thickness of sewing thread, sewing where the head meets the body, then repeating to make it extra secure. You don't need to flatten the head to the body at all – just sew where it is touching and the slipstitch will ensure that the stitches will not be seen.

9 Place the two pieces for each leg with right sides together. Pin, tack (baste) and machine stitch with a 5mm (¼in) seam, leaving the top of the leg open. Turn right side out and stuff.

10 Slipstitch the legs to the body, turning in 5mm (¼in) at the top of the leg. Sew right around the edges, forming a circle. Secure the thread to the body under the leg to start, and finish the stitching just under the top of the leg.

11 Place the tail sections with wrong sides together and use three strands of yellow embroidery thread (floss) to work blanket stitch around the edges, leaving the end open where it will join the body.

12 Stuff the tail lightly. Position it on the sheep's rear and sew on using three strands of yellow embroidery thread (floss) – work blanket stitch along the top of the tail, catching the tail to the body at the same time.

13 Slipstitch the gap in the sheep's tummy to close it, making sure she is still well stuffed! Remove any remaining tacking (basting) or pins.

Doggy Draught Excluder

This friendly dog will sit happily in front of the door, keeping out draughts, and you'll never have to tell him to 'Stay'. If you like, you can add some weight to his body and use him as a doorstop as well. Make him in colours to match the theme of the nursery.

Size

Approx 60cm (24in) long

You will need

Scraps of contrasting cotton fabric
1m (1⅛yd) of patterned cotton fabric
Tape measure
Erasable marker
Fabric scissors
Pins
Sewing needle
Sewing thread
Sewing machine
Toy stuffing
Gravel or dried beans (optional)
Small piece of fusible webbing
Pencil
Scrap of brown cotton fabric
Iron
Embroidery needle
Black embroidery thread (floss)

1 Use the templates (see page 122) to make pattern pieces and cut out the ears, legs and tail in the contrast cotton fabric. For the body, extend the length of the template until it measures about 60cm (24in). The pieces should include a seam allowance of 5mm (¼in). Cut out the body and the rear end circle from the patterned cotton.

2 Fold the body piece in half, with right sides together, matching the letters (A with A and B with B). Pin and tack (baste) **2** . Stitch together **10** along the underside of the body/ head (the long edge) and the angled edge of the top of the head, but leave the nose and tail ends open.

3 Run a gathering thread **24** (by hand is probably easier here) around the nose end, then draw up the stitches to close the gap and secure with a few stitches.

4 Turn the body the right way out and stuff firmly with toy stuffing. Run a gathering stitch right around the dog's rear end. Pull up the threads slightly, but do not tighten too much.

5 Pin the rear end circle over the dog's rear end. Turning in a 5mm (¼in) hem as you go, oversew **6** the circle securely to the body.

6 To make the appliqué **34** nose, place the fusible webbing over the template, paper side up, and trace the lines of the template. Cut out the shape roughly. Place the shape, paper side up, on the wrong side of the brown fabric. Iron for 3–4 seconds to fuse the webbing to the fabric. Cut out the shape accurately.

7 Peel off the backing paper and position the nose, coated side down, on the narrow end and pin (the top of the dog is the side with the small seam rather than the seam that goes all the way to the tail end). Oversew around the nose using three strands of embroidery thread (floss) – make small stitches with a fairly small space between each one. Secure the thread (floss) to the body under the nose to start, and finish the stitching just under the edge of the nose. To hide the end of the thread (floss), push the needle into the body and bring it out some distance away, so the thread (floss) is lost within the body.

Tip
If you want to add some weight to the draught excluder, you can put gravel or dried beans in the base of the body. If you do this – especially with gravel – I recommend that you use a double thickness of fabric for the body.

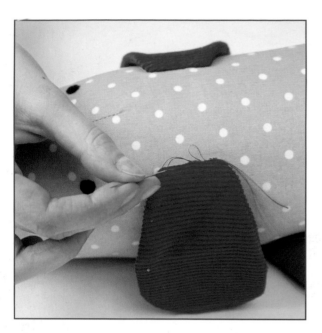

8 Place the ear pieces with right sides together and machine stitch around the edges with a 5mm (¼in) seam allowance, leaving a gap in the straight side for turning. Turn right side out. Turn the open edges to the inside and slipstitch **5** to close. Position the ears on the dog, using the photo for guidance, and oversew on firmly with a double thickness of thread. Secure the thread to the body under the ears to start, and finish the stitching under the ear, close to the top, so the stitches will be hidden.

9 Place the tail pieces with right sides together and machine stitch around the edges with a 5mm (¼in) seam, leaving the end that attaches to the body open. Turn right side out and stuff quite firmly. Repeat with the leg pieces.

Simple Skirt

This luxurious skirt is a good project to start with if you're new to sewing. There is no zip to insert – the waistband ties at the side, giving a stylish finish – and the ends of the ties cover the slit opening that allows you to pull on the skirt. The gathers add structure to the silky fabric and produce the lovely puffed shape of the design. Match with chunky knits and thick tights during the winter months, or a sheer blouse and hosiery for evening glamour. If you want to make it longer or shorter, add to or take away from the lower edge of the pattern.

Size

To fit size Small, Medium, Large (see page 121)

You will need

2m (2¼yd) of 112cm (45in) wide soft and silky fabric
    such as silk or synthetic satin
Pins
Tape measure
Tailor's chalk or erasable fabric marker
Fabric scissors
Sewing needle
Matching thread
50cm (20in) of 2cm (¾in) wide bias binding tape
Sewing machine
Iron
1m (1¼yd) of 2cm (¾in) wide elastic
Safety pins: 1 large, 1 medium

1 Cut out the fabric according to the pattern on page 124. Run gathering stitches **24** along the waist edge of the skirt. Pull up the stitches until the material is your exact waist measurement plus 1cm (⅜in) ease; wind the thread around a pin to secure.

2 Measure 15cm (6in) down from the waist on each side seam and mark. Stitch the side seam, as far as the marks, with a French seam **11**. The open part will form a slit at the top of the skirt.

3 Finish the slit by binding **28** each edge. Cut two pieces of bias binding tape, each 16cm (6¼in) long. Apply the binding to each side of the slit, folding in 1cm (⅜in) of binding at the lower end of the slit to neaten it. Press **16** each bound edge to the inside of the skirt.

4 Make the waistband by folding it in half with right sides together. Press. Press 1cm (⅜in) over to the wrong side on each long edge.

5 Open out the waistband and pin the skirt to one side with right sides and raw edges together, placing the skirt centrally on the waistband so that the two tie ends are equal. Stitch the gathered edge with a 1cm (⅜in) seam **10**.

6 Fold the waistband in half with right sides together. Pin, tack (baste) **2** and stitch along each short end and around to where it meets the skirt, with a 1cm (⅜in) seam. Trim the seam allowance, and trim the corners **13** diagonally. Clip into the seam allowance where the stitching ends.

7 Turn the waistband the right way out and press. On the inside of the skirt, remove any pins and then slipstitch **5** the folded edge of the waistband to the skirt to just cover the stitching line made in step 5. Press. Topstitch **7** along the lower edge of the waistband if you wish.

8 Make the hem, which also forms a casing **25** for the elastic: fold 4cm (1½in) to the inside of the skirt and press. Press under 1cm (⅜in) on the raw edge. Machine stitch along the folded edge of the casing, leaving a gap of about 5cm (2in) halfway along for inserting the elastic.

9 Fix a large safety pin to one end of the elastic and a smaller one to the other end. Start passing the smaller safety pin through the casing, using the large safety pin to anchor the other end. When the elastic is threaded through, overlap the ends and stitch together by hand or machine. Slipstitch the gap in the seam closed.

Tunic Dress

A summer dress in a classic vest shape – simple, striking and easy to wear. The design brings back happy childhood memories of long, sunny days and vibrant summer dresses. It is a very easy dress to make, because the neck and armholes are finished with bias binding tape. A tie belt adds definition to the waistline; it also features a contrasting fabric on the ends for a stylish twist. The skirt is knee-length; if you want it longer or shorter, add on to or take away from the hem edge of the pattern. The design works well in a bold pattern, as the front and back sections are each a single piece, so you can make the most of all those jazzy prints that are out there.

Size
To fit size Small, Medium, Large (see page 121)

You will need
Small and medium: 2.25m (2½yd) of 112cm (45in) wide cotton fabric
Large: 2.75m (3yd) of 112cm (45in) wide cotton fabric
Tape measure
Pins
Fabric scissors
Tailor's chalk or erasable fabric marker
Sewing machine
Sewing needle
Matching thread
Fabric scraps for the belt ends
3m (3¼yd) of 2cm (¾in) wide satin bias binding tape

1 Cut out the fabric according to the pattern pieces on page 123. Join the sides and shoulders of the dress with French seams **11**.

2 Make a hem by pressing 1cm (⅜in) to the inside at the bottom of the dress, then turn over the same amount again. Pin, tack (baste) **2** and topstitch **7**.

3 Apply bias binding **28** to the neck and armhole edges. When you turn the binding over the raw edge, hold it in place, then turn over the edge again so the binding is on the inside of the garment and doesn't show on the right side of the dress.

4 Make a tuck in the binding as you feed it around the V-shape of the neckline. Pin and tack (baste). Topstitch the binding in place close to the edge.

5 Fold a belt end in half with right sides together. Pin, tack (baste) and machine one side edge with a 1cm (⅜in) seam **10**. Press **16** the seam open with your fingers and pin the right side of the top of the belt end to the right side of the belt. Tack (baste) and stitch with a 1cm (⅜in) seam. Repeat at the other end of the belt.

6 Fold the main part of the belt in half with right sides together. Pin and tack (baste) from one end of the belt to the other. Machine with a 1cm (⅜in) seam, leaving a gap of 8cm (3¼in) for turning. Turn right side out. Slipstitch **5** the gap to close it.

Make-up Bag

This fun and easy make-up bag takes up very little fabric, so it is fantastic for using up those odd pieces of material that you have lying around. It's also a great opportunity to cut up old dresses in beautiful prints that you no longer wear but can't bear to part with. A make-up bag is an excellent gift, especially if you buy some items of make-up to put inside.

Size

Approx 20cm (8in) long × 10cm (4in) high

You will need

26 × 36cm (10¼ × 14¼in) of main fabric
26 × 36cm (10¼ × 14¼in) of lining fabric
Tape measure
Fabric scissors
Iron
Sewing needle
Thread to match fabric
Pins
Tailor's chalk or erasable fabric marker
17.5cm (7in) zip
Sewing machine with zip foot (optional)

1 Cut two pieces each 26 × 18cm (10¼ × 7⅛in) from the main fabric for the outer bag and two pieces each 26 × 18cm (10¼ × 7⅛in) of lining fabric. With the main fabric pieces right sides together, fold over 1.5cm (⅝in) to the wrong side along one long edge on both pieces and press **16** in place.

2 Open out the flaps again and tack (baste) **2** the two pieces together along the fold line. Open the seam flat and press.

3 Place the zip on top of the opened-out seam in the centre **43**. Make a chalk mark or mark with a pin at each end of the zip, where the zip teeth finish. Remove the zip from the fabric and put aside.

4 Transfer the mark you just made to the wrong side of the seam allowance flaps.

5 With the flaps together, sew a short seam **10** along the fold line from the edge of the fabric to approx 5mm (¼in) past the mark made in step 4. Repeat at the other end of the fold line.

6 Remove any pins. Open the fabric out flat, right side facing down, and press the seam allowance open.

7 Place the zip right side down on the centre of the seam allowance. The ends of the zip should slightly overlap the stitched sections of the seam made in step 5. Pin and tack (baste) the zip in place.

8 Remove any pins from the fabric. Turn the fabric over and, with the right side facing upward, take out the tacking (basting) stitches holding the seam together in the centre for around three-quarters of the length of the zip from the zip pull end.

9 Open the zip for around three-quarters of its length from the zip pull end.

10 Change the foot on your sewing machine for a zip foot (if you have one). With the zip side facing upward, sew the zip in place by sewing around all four sides. When you get to the zip pull, close it slightly to move it away from the needle so you don't have to stitch past it.

11 Take out the remaining tacking (basting) stitches and open the zip.

12 With the fabric right sides together, pin and sew the bottom and side seams.

13 Open out all the seams and press.

14 Put your hand into a bottom corner of the bag and open out the corner by spreading your fingers. Feel down with your other hand to match up the side and bottom seams at the corner. When one seam is directly on top of the other, place a pin across the corner to hold it in place.

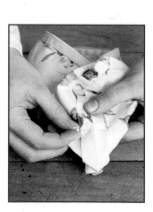

15 Place the corner on a flat surface and measure 3cm (1¼in) down the seamline from the corner, then place a pin marker.

16 At the pin marker, using a ruler, mark the sewing line across the corner with tailor's chalk or pencil. It should be approx 7.5cm (3in) in length. Pin and sew **7** along the marker line. Take out pins.

17 Repeat steps 14–16 on the other corner.

18 Trim off the excess fabric at the corners **13** with pinking shears.

19 With the lining fabric right sides together, pin and sew the side and bottom seams, leaving the top open. Repeat steps 13–18 as for the main fabric.

20 Fold over the top edge by approx 1.5cm (⅝in) and press. Slip the lining inside the main piece with wrong sides together, easing it in place carefully. Pin the top edge of the lining along the zip, a short distance from the teeth (sometimes it's easier to turn the bag inside out to pin the lining in place). Slipstitch **5** the top edge of the lining in place.

Embellishing

As well as making items from scratch, this section covers embellishing ready-made items, such as a plain towel or cushion. Embroidery and appliqué are great ways to add your own unique look to plain purchased items – and will make them look more expensive than they really were.

Embroidered Tablecloth and Napkins

Even a very beginner will be able to make this tablecloth and matching napkins. It's an ideal project to give as a gift because it looks impressive, but takes only basic sewing knowledge. Both tablecloth and napkins are hemmed in a straight line and the strawberry is embroidered using very simple and basic embroidery stitches.

Size

Tablecloth: to fit the table
Napkins: 33cm (13in) square

You will need

Enough fabric to cover the table, allowing for a 25cm (10in) drop plus a 1.5cm (⅝in) seam allowance on each side

Bobble trim: measure the length and the width of your tablecloth, add together and multiply by two for the length of trim required

Tape measure

Fabric scissors

Sewing needle

Embroidery thread (floss) in red, green and white

Embroidery hoop

Embroidery needle

Thread to match fabric and trim

1 Measure the table and add 53cm (21¼in) to both the length and the width for the drop and the seam allowances all round. Cut the fabric to size. Cut six 36cm (14¼in) squares for the napkins.

2 Turn over the edges of the tablecloth by 5mm (¼in) and then by 1cm (⅜in), pin in place and then hem **18** with a straight stitch. Repeat on the napkins. Press **16** the hems.

Tip
Depending on the width of the fabric that you buy, a 75cm (30in) length should be enough for about six napkins.

3 Pin and sew the bobble trim around all the edges of the tablecloth only.

4 Trace a suitable embroidery motif onto tracing paper. Turn the tracing paper over and draw around the lines on the back with a soft pencil. Turn the tracing paper over again and position the motif in one corner of one of the napkins. Go over the lines again with a sharp pencil to transfer the design to the fabric of the napkin. Repeat on all napkins and in each corner of the tablecloth.

5 Hand embroider the motifs in each corner of the tablecloth and on one corner of each napkin. Here we have stitched strawberries to tie in with the bobble fringe, using a simple satin stitch **31** for the strawberry, French knots **32** for the pips and three lazy daisy stitches **30** for the leaves.

Whale Towel

This very simple and satisfying project is a great way to jazz up a plain towel – and it will make bath time more fun. You can adjust the pattern for a bigger towel by making the background strips longer and adding more whales – your whole family could have matching towels, all in different colours.

Size
Standard towel

You will need
Plain towel in a pale colour
Blue cotton fabric a little wider than the width of
    towel × 25cm (10in) deep
Erasable fabric marker
Tape measure
Scraps of patterned cotton fabric
Pencil
Approx 40cm (16in) of fusible webbing
Fabric scissors
Iron
Sewing machine with a freehand foot and a
    zigzag foot
Sewing thread in colours to contrast with the fabric
Embroidery needle
Embroidery thread (floss) in black and blue
Iron-on transfer pen (optional)

1 Take the fabric for the sea and draw two rectangles side by side, with a small gap between them, using the fabric marker. Make each rectangle the width of the towel by 7cm (2¾in) deep.

2 To make the appliqué **34** , place the webbing over the template on page 125, paper side up, and trace the lines of the whale and water spurt templates several times. Cut out the shapes roughly. The towel shown features seven whales at each end (one set facing to the left and one set facing to the right), but you may need more or fewer whales depending on the size of your towel.

3 Place each shape, paper side up, on the wrong side of the appropriate fabric. Iron for around 3–4 seconds to fuse in place. Cut out around the shapes accurately.

4   Peel off the backing paper and arrange the whales, coated side down, on the right side of the sea background (use the photo for guidance on positioning). Position a spurt of water over each whale's head, tucking the tip slightly under the top edge of the head. Iron in place to fuse and leave the motifs to cool.

5   Using the freehand foot, machine stitch **7** carefully around each motif just inside the edge.

6   Backstitch **4** the whales' facial features using three strands of black embroidery thread (floss), and make French knots **32** for the eyes. If you prefer to have a drawn line to follow, use an erasable fabric marker or an iron-on transfer pen.

7   Embroider splashes around the spurts, using three strands of blue embroidery thread (floss) and working a few satin stitches **31** over each other to make the water drop shapes.

8   Place a piece of webbing, paper side up, on the wrong side of each sea background piece. Iron for 3–4 seconds as before and then leave to cool. Peel off the backing paper.

9   Cut out each sea background: it should measure the width of the towel × 7cm (2¾in) deep.

10   Position each strip of whales at each end of the towel. The base of the whales should face the edge of the towel. Iron in place and leave to cool.

11   Machine stitch around each strip using a zigzag stitch **9**. The towel is ready to make bath time fun!

Colonial Cushion

Scatter cushions (throw pillows) are a great way to introduce an accent colour into a colour scheme, or to quickly change the style of a room. Plain cushions in a range of colours are easily available and inexpensive, but create your own unique look by making this vintage-style cover to go over the top. You could also use this cover over a plain-coloured version of the basic cushion on page 54, omitting its appliqué details.

Size
To fit a 40cm (16in) square cushion

You will need
50cm (20in) of 112cm (45in) wide cream linen fabric
1.25m (1½yd) of 5cm (2in) wide cotton insertion lace
Tape measure
Fabric scissors
Sewing machine or sewing needle
Cream thread
40cm (16in) square plain colour cushion (pillow)

1   Measure and cut the following pieces from the cream linen: one rectangle 27 × 43cm (10½ × 17¼in), one rectangle 33 × 43cm (13 × 17¼in) and one 19cm (7½in) square. Measure a border frame 10.5cm (4¼in) wide all around the square piece and then cut out the 22cm (8¾in) square from the centre. Cut the square from the centre down to an 18cm (7⅛in) square.

2   Zigzag **9** around all the raw edges to prevent the pieces from fraying. With the fabric wrong side up, press **16** a 5mm (¼in) seam allowance around all the inner edges of the border frame, snipping carefully into the inner corners up to the fold point so the seam allowance will press flat.

3   Turn the border frame over right side upward. Pin the lace around the inside of the frame. Start at one corner and fold the lace at a right angle to the back of the work at each corner. Tack (baste) **2** and remove the pins.

4   Stitch **7** the lace in place from the wrong side, making sure you catch the edge of the lace and the seam allowance – but not the right angle folded corners of the lace – as you work.

5   Zigzag stitch diagonally across the folded lace at one corner. Pull the threads to the back of the work and knot securely. Repeat at each corner.

6 Using small, sharp scissors, carefully trim away the folded corner of the lace on the wrong side along the diagonal stitching, making sure you do not cut through any of the stitching.

7 Trim the centre square if necessary to fit the inside edge of the lace, allowing an extra 1cm (⅜in) all round. Press the raw edge of the centre square over to the wrong side by 5mm (¼in) all round. Pin the inside edge of the lace to overlap the edge of the square on the right side. Stitch the lace to the centre square.

8 Make a 5cm (2in) double hem along one long edge of each linen rectangle. Either machine stitch **18** or hand stitch **19** each hem in place.

9 With right sides up, pin the two rectangles with the hems overlapping to make a 43cm (17¼in) square. With right sides together, pin this square to the front of the cover. Machine stitch **10** around all four edges with a 1.5cm (⅝in) seam allowance.

10 Turn the cover right side out through the hole in the back and press. Insert the cushion (pillow) through the envelope back to finish.

Teddy Hat

This hat is practical as well as very cute. It will keep baby's head warm when out and about, and makes fun at-home loungewear! It will make a great present for a new baby, and the neutral colours mean it is suitable for a boy or a girl.

Size
To fit a baby up to 6 months

You will need
50cm (20in) of 150cm (60in) wide fleece fabric
Scraps of patterned cotton fabric
Erasable marker and iron-on transfer pen
Tape measure
Fabric scissors
15cm (6in) square of fusible webbing
Pencil
Pins
Sewing needle
Sewing thread to match fabric
Sewing machine
Embroidery needle
Stranded embroidery thread (floss) in black
    and yellow

1   Use the templates on page 126 to cut out the hat pieces, outer ears and band from the fleece, and two inner ears from the cotton fabric. The pieces should include a seam allowance of 5mm (¼in). Use an erasable fabric marker to mark the positions of the ears on one of the hat pieces.

2   For the appliqué **34**, place the webbing over the muzzle template, paper side up, and trace the lines. Cut out the shape roughly and place paper side up on the wrong side of the cotton fabric. Iron for 3–4 seconds to fuse in place. Cut out the muzzle accurately. Remove the backing paper.

3   Place the outer and inner ear with right sides together, pin and tack (baste) **2**. Machine stitch around each ear with a 5mm (¼in) seam **10**, leaving the base open. Cut triangular notches out of the seam allowance **12** to reduce bulk. Turn the ears right side out and press **16** with your fingers.

4   Lay one hat piece with right side uppermost. With raw edge to raw edge, position each ear as marked on the template, with raw edges aligned and the ear lying over the hat. Pin and tack (baste).

5   Place the two hat pieces with right sides together. Machine stitch around the hat with a 5mm (¼in) seam, sewing in the ears and leaving the base open.

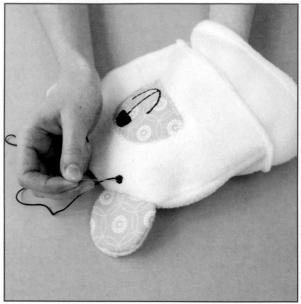

6 Make a hem  19 along one long edge of the band. With right sides together, stitch across the short ends with a 5mm (¼in) seam. Press the seam open with your fingers. Pin the raw edge of the band to the base of the hat, right side of band to wrong side of hat. Make sure that the band's seam is at the back of the hat (inner ears are on the front of the hat). Tack (baste) and machine stitch in place.

7 Use the iron-on transfer pen to transfer the nose and mouth lines to the muzzle. Using six strands of black embroidery thread (floss), backstitch **4** the line under the nose and along the mouth. Embroider the nose using satin stitch **31**.

8 Oversew **6** the muzzle to the hat using three strands of yellow embroidery thread (floss). Make small stitches with a fairly small space between each one. (The motif is not ironed into position, as the heat would flatten the surrounding fleece.)

9 Using six strands of black embroidery thread (floss), backstitch a circle for each eye and then fill it in using two layers of satin stitch to give a more padded effect.

10 Fold the band to the right side of the hat to create the turn-up.

Toy Tidy

A toy tidy will encourage toddlers to put away their toys without too much fuss! The cord pockets are durable, so lots of things can be stuffed inside. Hang this tidy from the back of a door, or set two small hooks in the perfect place on the wall. If your child has a favourite animal, use that as inspiration for a single motif, repeated in different colours and patterns.

Size
80 × 60cm (31½ × 24in)

You will need
1.75m (2yd) of 112cm (45in) wide striped cotton fabric
Metre ruler and set square
Erasable fabric marker
Fabric scissors
75cm (30in) of 112cm (45in) wide corduroy fabric
40 × 60cm (16 x 24in) of fusible webbing
Pencil
Iron
Scraps of patterned cotton fabric
Sewing machine with freehand foot and zigzag foot
Sewing thread
Iron-on transfer pen (optional)
Embroidery thread (floss) in black
Embroidery needle
Pins

1 Cut two pieces each 83 × 63cm (33 × 25in) for the front and back from the striped fabric, with the stripes running vertically.

2 Cut twelve rectangles, each 23 × 25cm (9 × 10in), from the corduroy for the six pockets.

3 For the appliqué **34**, place the webbing over the animal templates on page 127, paper side up, and trace the different shapes of the template. Cut out the shapes roughly. Place each shape, paper side up, on the wrong side of the appropriate fabric. For the sheep's head and legs, and the rabbit's and cat's inner ears, use a fabric that contrasts with the body. Iron for 3–4 seconds to fuse. Cut out the shapes accurately.

4 Peel off the backing paper from the animals and arrange the bodies, adhesive side down, on the right side of six of the pocket pieces (the longer sides are top and bottom). Iron in place to fuse and leave to cool. Attach other parts, such as the sheep's face and legs (tuck the ends under the body) and details such as the inner ears, in the same way.

5 Using the freehand foot, machine stitch around each animal, just inside the edge, using a straight stitch **7**. Repeat to highlight other features on the animals, as shown in the photos. A thread in a contrasting colour looks good. You can backstitch **4** these pieces if you prefer, or sew with running stitch **3**.

6 If you wish, use an erasable fabric marker or iron-on transfer pen to mark the facial features on each creature. Using six strands of black embroidery thread (floss), stitch the mouths using backstitch, make French knots **32** for the eyes (satin stitch **31** for the eyes on the rabbit and pig), and satin stitch for the noses on the dog and cat. For nostrils, use cross stitch **33** on the pig and backstitch on the sheep.

Tip
If you want a larger tidy, make the main pieces bigger and add extra pockets, repeating the animals as necessary.

7 Place the back and front of each pocket with right sides together, and pin and tack (baste) **2**. Machine stitch around the edges with a 1.5cm (⅝in) seam **10**, leaving a small gap along the bottom for turning right side out.

8 Turn all the pockets right side out and press **16**. Slipstitch **5** the edges of the gaps to close them. Position the pockets on the striped front piece, roughly 6cm (2½in) from all the edges – this includes a 1.5cm (⅝in) seam allowance for attaching the front piece to the back. Make sure that the pockets are straight, with a gap of 5cm (2in) between each pair of pockets, horizontally and vertically.

9 Pin and tack (baste) the pockets in place. Machine stitch around the sides and bottom, leaving the top open, using zigzag stitch **9** in a colour matched to the animal on the pocket.

10 To make the hangers for the top of the tidy, cut two rectangles of striped fabric, each 27 × 9cm (10½ × 3½in). Fold in half lengthways, with right sides together, and sew along the long edge with a 1.5cm (⅝in) seam. Turn inside out and press. Referring to the photo above, fold each piece into a handle with a straight top. Insert pins at the corners to hold the handle in shape.

11 Place the hangers on the front of the tidy, with raw edges together and the hanger lying against the front of the tidy, and roughly lining up the outer edges with the outer edge of the pockets. Pin and tack (baste).

12 Take the back piece of the tidy and pin it to the front, right sides together. Sew right around the edges with a 1.5cm (⅝in) seam, leaving a gap along the bottom edge that is big enough for turning the tidy.

13 Turn the tidy right side out, pushing out each edge fully. Press the edges. Slipstitch the gap to close it, and the tidy is ready to store favourite toys.

Extending Skills

The projects in this section are rather bigger than most of the others in the book, so may require a little more time to make. They still rely on basic techniques, although they have additional elements to consider – such as matching pattern repeats on the curtains or cording the blind.

Striped Duvet Cover

Covers for duvets are straightforward to make and this allows you a free choice of fabric to complement your decorative scheme. This reversible cover uses a simple design for a contemporary style, but your choice of fabric could make it look very different.

Size
224cm (88in) square

You will need
2.75m (3yd) of 137cm (54in) wide white fabric
4m (4½yd) of 137cm (54in) wide coloured fabric
Tape measure
Fabric scissors
Pins
Sewing machine
Sewing thread to match fabrics
Iron
4.6m (5yd) of 137cm (54in) wide patterned
    backing fabric
9m (10yd) piping cord

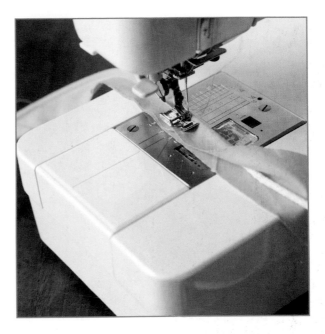

1   Cut four stripes of white fabric and five stripes of coloured fabric each 27cm (10½in) wide and 226cm (88¾in) long. Pin and then machine stitch **10** the strips right sides together in alternate order with a 1cm (⅜in) seam allowance, beginning with a coloured strip.

2   Gently press **16** all the seam allowances to one side, towards the coloured strip.

3   Working from the right side, topstitch **7** on the coloured fabric 5mm (¼in) from the join to hold all the seam allowances in place.

4   Cut bias strips **27** 5cm (2in) wide from the remaining coloured fabric and join them to make a continuous strip at least 9m (10yd) long. Fold the strip in half with wrong sides together and slip the piping cord **37** right into the fold. Machine stitch along the strip as close to the cord as possible, using the zip foot on the machine.

5   For the ties, cut six strips from the coloured fabric and six from the white fabric each 5cm (2in) wide and 47cm (18½in) long. Fold each strip in half lengthways, wrong sides together, and then turn the raw edges into the middle down the long side and at the ends. Topstitch along all four sides to make six 2cm (¾in) wide ties in each fabric.

6 Pin the piping all around the edge of the top side of the cover on the right side with raw edges aligned and the cord of the piping on the inward side. Pin six matching ties over the piping along the bottom edge of the cover at 25cm (10in) intervals, with the raw ends aligned with the raw edge and the ties lying over the cover top. At the corners, snip into the piping seam allowance only almost to the stitching so the piping will lie neatly around the corner.

Tips

If your fabric is narrower than 137cm (54in) you will need more to cut the strips. The five strips need a width of at least 135cm (52½in).

For the reverse of the cover you may be able to find a suitable quilt backing fabric, which is available extra wide so you will need less fabric.

7 For the facing, cut a strip 10cm (4in) wide and 226cm (88¾in) long from the remaining white fabric. Make a narrow double hem **18** along one long edge. Pin, tack (baste) **2** and stitch the unhemmed edge of the facing over the piping and ties with right sides together. Turn right side out and press in place.

8 Cut the reverse side of the cover to match the top side, seaming two lengths of fabric together to make the full width. Repeat steps 6 and 7, omitting the piping, to add matching ties and a facing to the bottom edge of the reverse side of the duvet cover.

9 Pin the top to the reverse, with right sides together and with the piping between them on the inside. Stitch the three unfaced sides using a zipper foot, stitching as close to the cording as possible. Take extra care at the corners.

10 Zigzag **9** the raw edges of all the seams on three sides. Turn the duvet cover right side out and press.

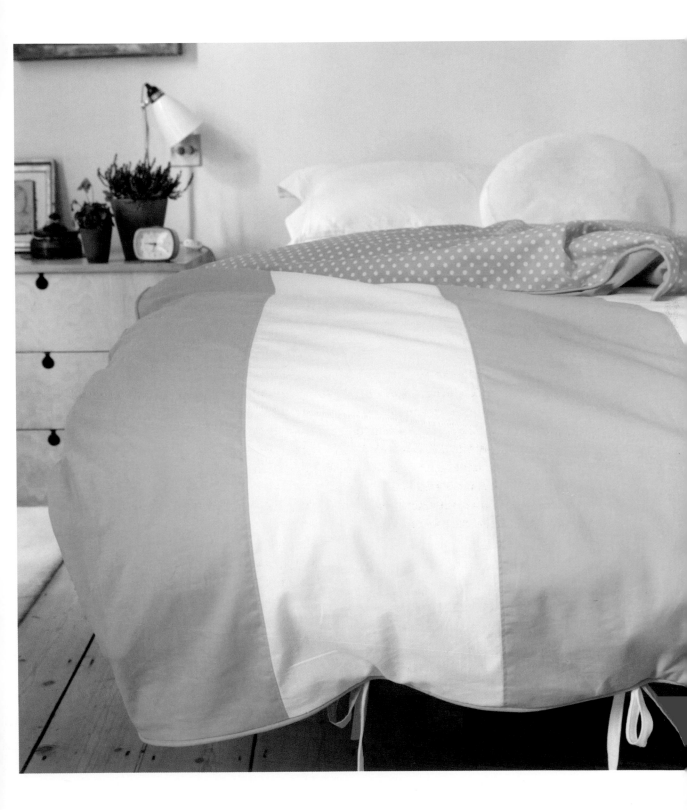

Playmat

This cheerful playmat can be used as a baby quilt or can provide a warm, soft layer on the floor for the baby to play or sleep on during the day. It's made from squares pieced together and appliquéd with cute dinosaurs. The measurements have been calculated to ensure the pieces fit together properly using either the metric or imperial system – use either one or the other but do not try to combine them.

Size
80 × 105cm (32 × 42in)

You will need

75cm (30in) square of neutral fabric

Tape measure

Fabric scissors

35cm (14in) of each of 7 different patterned fabrics

35cm (14in) square of each of 3 different plain fabrics

120 × 130cm (48 × 52in) of plain backing fabric

Pencil

Iron

50cm (20in) fusible webbing

Embroidery needle

Stranded embroidery thread (floss) in colours to contrast with the fabrics

Sewing machine

Sewing threads in colours to match the fabrics

100cm (40in) square of 56g (2oz) polyester wadding (batting)

1   Cut twelve rectangles, each 15 × 20cm (6½ × 8½in) from the neutral fabric. Cut three rectangles, each 15 × 10.5cm (6½ × 4½in), from each plain fabric and from the backing fabric. Cut four 15 × 10.5cm (6½ × 4½in) rectangles from each patterned fabric.

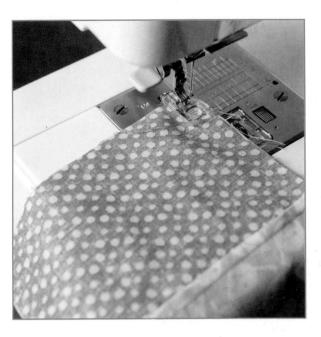

2   To make the appliqué 34 , copy the template pieces on page 128 and trace each piece two times on the paper side of the fusible webbing. Reverse the shapes and trace each piece another two times for the dinosaurs facing the other way. Choose different colours for the different pieces, using the photograph as a guide, and fuse the shapes onto the wrong side of the appropriate fabric.

3   Cut out the fused shape and peel off the backing paper. Position the two pieces to make up a dinosaur in the centre of each square of cream fabric, right side up. Fuse the shape to the square using the iron.

4   Hand embroider around each shape in the design using running stitch 3 , blanket stitch 29 and chain stitch 30 using three strands of embroidery thread (floss) in a contrasting colour to the shape.

5   Embroider the eye of each dinosaur in backstitch 4 and add further stitched details if you wish.

6   Pair up the small fabric rectangles, moving them around until you are happy with the combinations – you will have more than you need so can add and remove rectangles to suit.

7   Using the diagram on page 110, place the paired rectangles and the appliqué squares in rows to make up the playmat, moving them around until you are happy with the arrangement.

8   Pick up the pieces from the first row in order and place the first two right sides together. Stitch together along one edge with a 5mm (¼in) seam 16 . Repeat to make up the row. Make the other rows in the same way, then press 17 all the seams flat towards the darker fabric.

9   Stitch the rows together in order in the same way, matching the cross seams 14 , to make up the front of the playmat.

Diagram = Stitch together the pieces from the first row in order and then make up the other four rows in the same way, keeping the arrangement of blocks as set. Join the five rows together in order to make up the playmat.

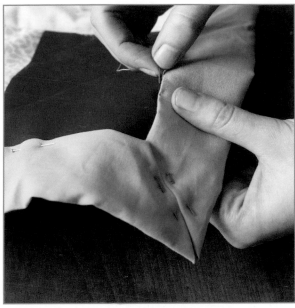

10 Lay the backing fabric right side down on a flat surface and centre the wadding (batting) on top. Lay the playmat front on top, right side up, making sure it is centred on the backing and wadding (batting). Pin and then tack (baste) **2** the three layers together securely so they will not move. Machine stitch **7** along all the seams of the playmat to quilt the three layers together.

11 Trim the wadding (batting) to an equal 4cm (1½in) larger than the playmat front all round. Trim the raw edge of the backing if necessary so it is an equal 10cm (4in) larger than the playmat front all round. Fold the backing over the wadding (batting) to the front of the mat, enclosing the raw edges and forming a wide border around the front edge. Turn under the raw edge of the backing by 1cm (⅜in) all round and pin in place, folding the corners neatly. Slipstitch **5** or machine stitch the binding in place to finish.

Tab-headed Curtain

Shaped tabs with a button fastening give this easy curtain an extra decorative touch. An alternative design would be to stitch long, thin ties into the seam, which can then be tied in bows over the pole.

Measuring for curtains

The finished drop measures from the top of the pole or the bottom of the curtain track to 4cm (1½in) below the csill (or to the floor for floor-length curtains).

The finished width is the length of the curtain track for each curtain.

You will need

Main fabric length: finished drop plus seam
   allowances of 13.5cm (5⅛in)
Main fabric width: finished curtain width plus seam
   allowances of 10cm (4in)
Lining: 10cm (4in) shorter and narrower than the
   main fabric
Strip of lead weights to match the hem of each
   curtain (optional)
Buttons
Tape measure
Pins
Thread
Fabric scissors
Iron
Cardboard for template

1 For each tab cut two pieces of fabric measuring 22 × 6cm (8½ × 2½in) along the straight grain.

2 Cut a simple template from the cardboard to the finished size of the intended tab. Place the template in the exact centre of a fabric strip on the wrong side and draw around it, then add at least 1.5cm (⅝ in) seam allowance around the sides and point.

3 Machine stitch **10** the tabs in pairs with right sides together along the template marking, leaving the flat end open. Trim the seam allowance down to 2mm (¹⁄₁₆in) around each tab.

4 Turn each tab right side out, easing out the corners by gently pushing each one out with the tip of a crochet hook or a chopstick. Press **16** each tab flat.

5 Lay the main fabric out on the work surface, wrong side up. Turn back 5cm (2in) along each side seam and pin in place.

6 Turn up 12cm (4½in) at the hem and pin. Make a mitre **36** at each bottom corner. Slipstitch **5** the hem in place, making sure the stitches do not show on the right side. If the curtain fabric is lightweight, add a strip of lead weights inside the hem before sewing.

7 Lay out the lining on the work surface, wrong side up. Turn back 5cm (2in) along each side seam and pin in place. Turn up 12cm (4½in) at the hem and pin. Make a mitre at each bottom corner. Machine **18** or slipstitch the hem in place.

8 Place the lining wrong sides together to the curtain and pin in place down each side and along the bottom. Slipstitch the lining to the hem at the sides and bottom of the main curtain.

> **Tip**
> If you are using patterned fabric with a repeat and need to join widths to make up the width of your curtain, see page 14 for how to calculate how much extra fabric is needed to match the repeats across the seam.

9 With the curtain right side up, pin the tabs in place so they are evenly spaced along the top edge, with the tab pointing downward. Cut a heading strip 8cm (3¼in) wide and 6cm (2½in) longer than the stitched curtain width.

10 Turn up 1.5cm (⅝in) along one long edge of the heading strip. Place the heading strip on the top of the main curtain with right sides together, enclosing the tabs between the layers, and with raw edges aligned. Pin and tack (baste) **2** , then machine stitch along the top edge with a 1.5cm (⅝in) seam allowance.

11 Fold the heading strip over onto the curtain lining and fold in the extra fabric at each end to finish. Slipstitch the folded lower edge of the heading to the lining.

12 Bring the tabs over to the front of the curtain and sew the buttons **41** in place through all layers of fabric to make the loops.

Roman Blind

Roman blinds are suitable for most window styles, except those more than 150cm (60in) wide or inward-opening casements. They look neat and work particularly well where there is no room to hang curtains at the sides of a window. Choose fabric with a simple design – strong geometrics like stripes and checks work well, as do small-scale patterns that do not become a mess of shapes when the blind is up. Fabrics with some crispness and body work best.

Measuring for a blind

Blinds are usually mounted inside the window recess or outside the recess on the face of the wall.

Inside the recess:

The finished drop is the measurement from the top of the recess to the top of the sill

The finished width is the measurement from one side of the recess to the other

On the wall:

The finished drop is the measurement from the top of the fixing to 10cm (4in) below the sill

The finished width is the width of the window opening plus at least 5cm (2in) on each side

You will need

Main fabric length: finished drop plus 20cm (8in) for hem and top

Main fabric width: finished width plus 10cm (4in) for side hems

Lining: as for main fabric, plus one strip for each rod casing measuring 12cm (4½in) deep by the width of the blind plus 4cm (1½in)

1 dowel rod for each rod casing

2.5 × 5cm (1 × 2in) strip of wood cut to the finished
    blind width

3 small brass or plastic rings for each rod casing

4 screw eyes

3 lengths of cord, each twice the finished drop of the
    blind plus the finished width

1 drop weight

1   Lay out the main fabric right side downward. Turn
a 5cm (2in) hem to the wrong side at the bottom and
along each side. Press **16**, making sure the corners
are square.

2   To make the mitred corners **36**, unfold the
pressed hems and turn in each corner so the diagonal
fold is at the point where the side and bottom creases
intersect. Press the corners.

3   Turn the side and bottom hems again so the
diagonal folds meet. Slipstitch **5** the diagonal folds
together. Repeat at the other bottom corner.

4   Slipstitch the raw edges of the side and bottom
hems to secure them in place, making quite large
stitches on the reverse of the blind but keeping
stitches on the right side of the fabric tiny so they
are invisible.

5   Lay out the lining right side downward. Turn a
6cm (2½in) hem to the wrong side at the bottom
and along each side and pin. Pin the lining to the
main fabric along the sides and bottom with wrong
sides together, so 1cm (⅜in) of the main fabric shows
around the lining. Slipstitch in place along the sides
and the bottom.

6   Fold each casing strip in half lengthwise with
wrong sides together. Turn the raw edges over twice
by 1cm (⅜in) to form a double hem and press in
place. Machine stitch along both long edges **7**
of the hem.

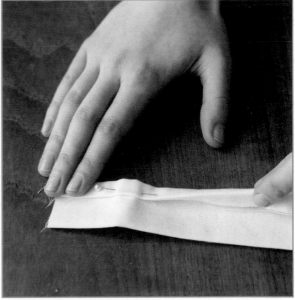

7 Use a pencil to mark the position of the rod casings on the lining side of the blind. Pin each casing in place along the pencil marks.

8 Stitch the casing through all the layers. Work as close to the edges of each as possible, removing pins as you go.

9 Insert a dowel rod into each casing of the blind. Turn in the open end of each casing and slipstitch it securely to lock the dowel in.

10 Oversew [6] a ring 2.5cm (1in) in from one side of the bottom casing, then repeat to sew a ring to each casing in line with the first ring. Repeat to attach a row of rings along the other side of the blind, then add a row up the middle. Measure carefully before you attach each ring.

11 Staple the top raw edge of the blind to one side of the wooden lath and roll the top of the blind over to completely cover the wood. Mark the position of the rows of rings on the lath. Screw the eyes through the fabric into the wood at the top of each row. Add the fourth eye just in from the edge from which the cords will be hung.

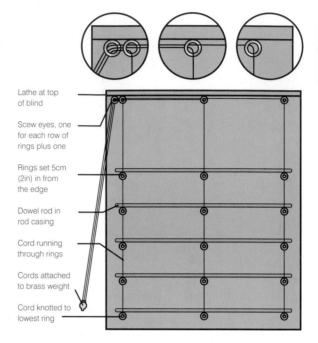

Lathe at top of blind

Scew eyes, one for each row of rings plus one

Rings set 5cm (2in) in from the edge

Dowel rod in rod casing

Cord running through rings

Cords attached to brass weight

Cord knotted to lowest ring

12 Tie one length of cord to the bottom ring on one side. Thread it up through the row of rings and the eye. Repeat to cord the other rows of rings – see the cording diagram above. At the top, thread the lengths through the eyes towards the extra eye. Take them all through the extra eye, but do not cut off yet.

13 Lay the blind flat with the cords straight. Thread the loose end of the cords through the weight and knot them so the weight is level with the bottom of the blind. Trim the ends of the cord. The blind is now ready to hang.

Shoulder Bag

Use at 600%

The following seam allowances are included:
Bag: 1cm (³/₈in)
Pocket: 1cm (³/₈in)

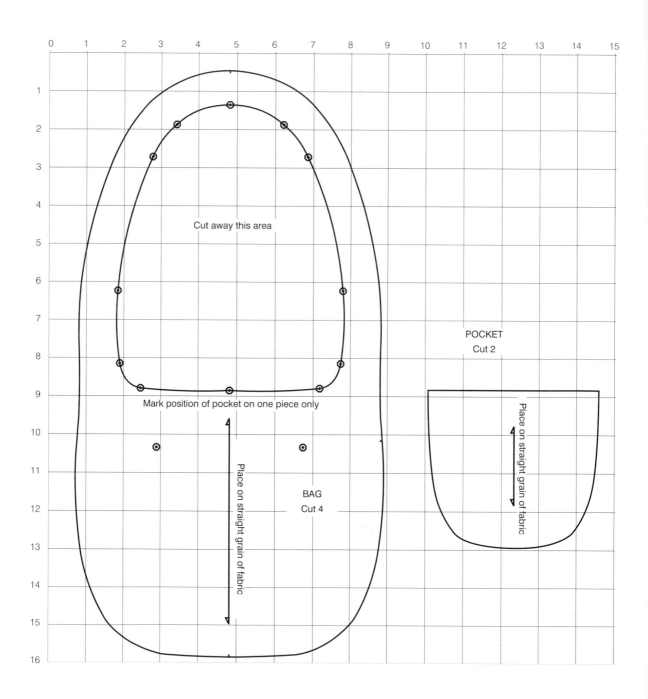

Cut away this area

POCKET
Cut 2

Mark position of pocket on one piece only

Place on straight grain of fabric

BAG
Cut 4

Place on straight grain of fabric

Lace Bow Top

Use at 600%

The following seam allowances are included:
Shoulder seam: 1.5cm (³/₈in)
Side seams: 1.5cm (³/₈in)
Neck and armhole: 1.2cm (½in)
Hem: 2cm (¾in)

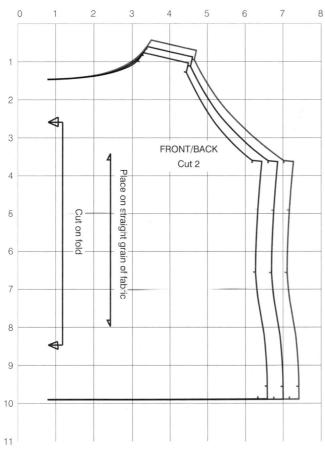

The patterns for the garments in this book are in three sizes:
Small (approx. UK size 8–10/US size 4–6)
Medium (approx. UK size 12–14/US size 8–10)
Large (approx. UK size 16–18/US size 12–14)

The small size is printed in black, the medium in red, and the large in blue.

Doggy Draught Excluder

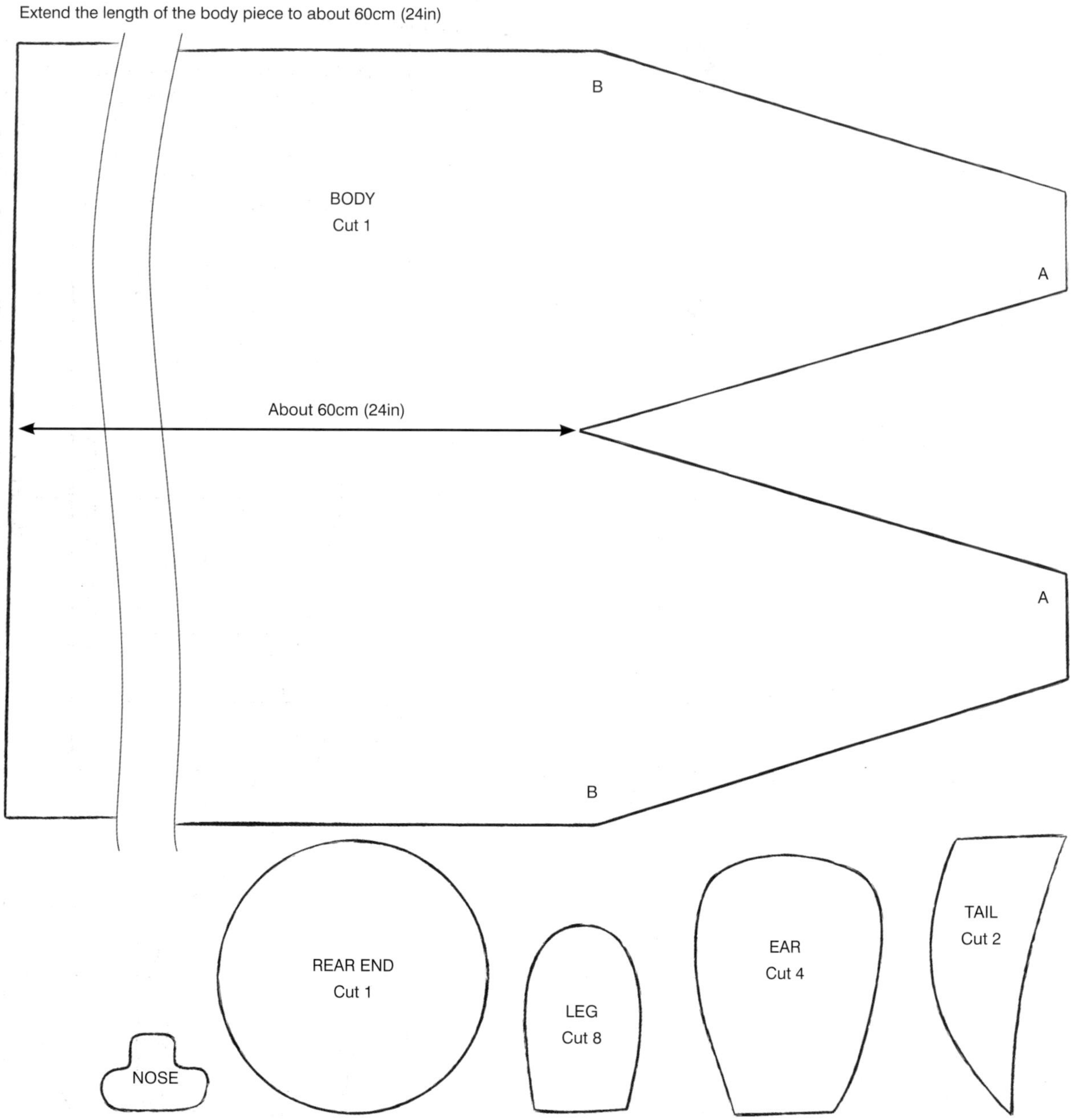

Extend the length of the body piece to about 60cm (24in)

B

BODY
Cut 1

A

About 60cm (24in)

A

B

NOSE

REAR END
Cut 1

LEG
Cut 8

EAR
Cut 4

TAIL
Cut 2

Use at 250%

Tunic Dress

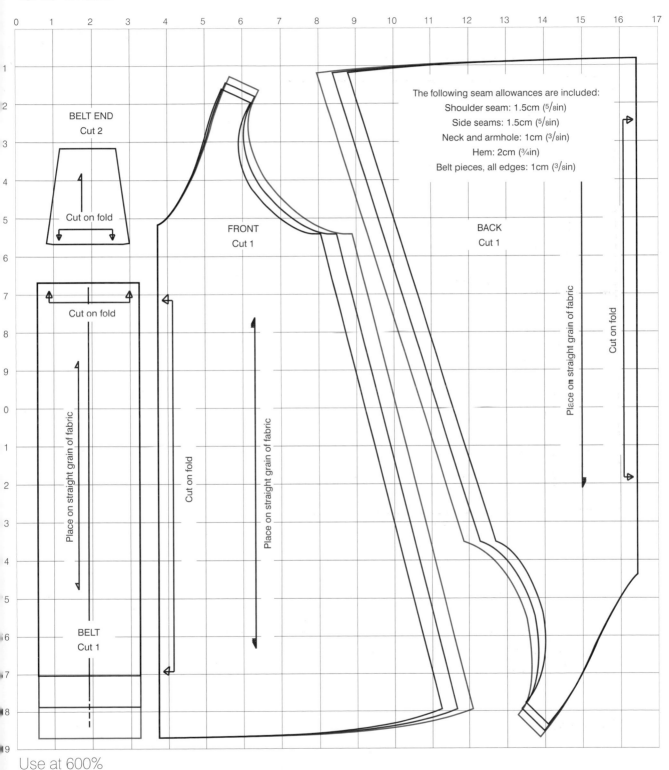

BELT END
Cut 2

Cut on fold

FRONT
Cut 1

BACK
Cut 1

The following seam allowances are included:
Shoulder seam: 1.5cm (5/8in)
Side seams: 1.5cm (5/8in)
Neck and armhole: 1cm (3/8in)
Hem: 2cm (3/4in)
Belt pieces, all edges: 1cm (3/8in)

Place on straight grain of fabric

Cut on fold

Place on straight grain of fabric

Cut on fold

Cut on fold

Place on straight grain of fabric

BELT
Cut 1

Use at 600%

Simple Skirt

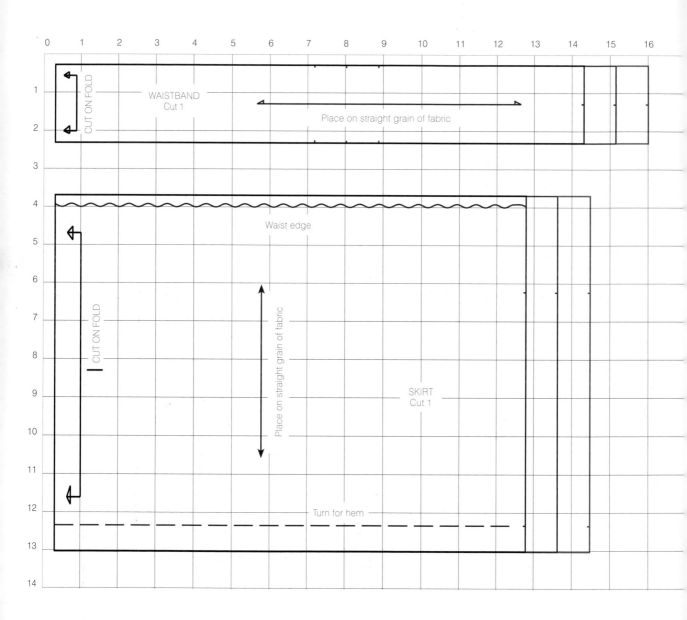

WAISTBAND
Cut 1

CUT ON FOLD

Place on straight grain of fabric

Waist edge

CUT ON FOLD

Place on straight grain of fabric

SKIRT
Cut 1

Turn for hem

Use at 600%

Whale Towel

Use at 100%

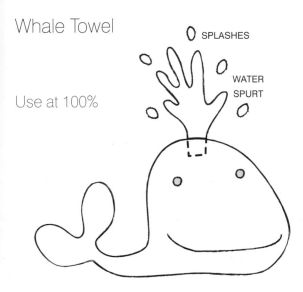

SPLASHES

WATER
SPURT

Olivia the Sheep

When cutting out each pair of pieces for the ears, legs and tail, and the two
pieces for the back of the head, one of the pieces needs to be reversed.

Use at 250%

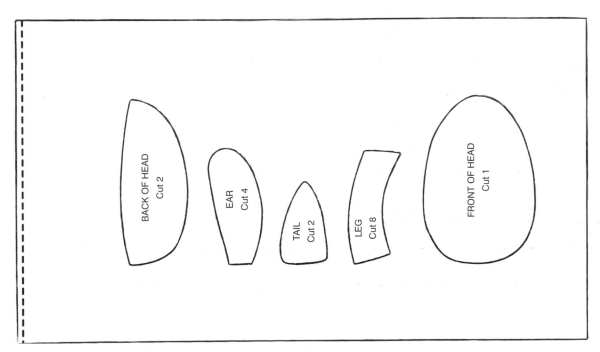

BACK OF HEAD
Cut 2

EAR
Cut 4

TAIL
Cut 2

LEG
Cut 8

FRONT OF HEAD
Cut 1

Teddy Hat

Use at 250%

When cutting out each pair of
outer and inner ears, one of the
pieces needs to be reversed.

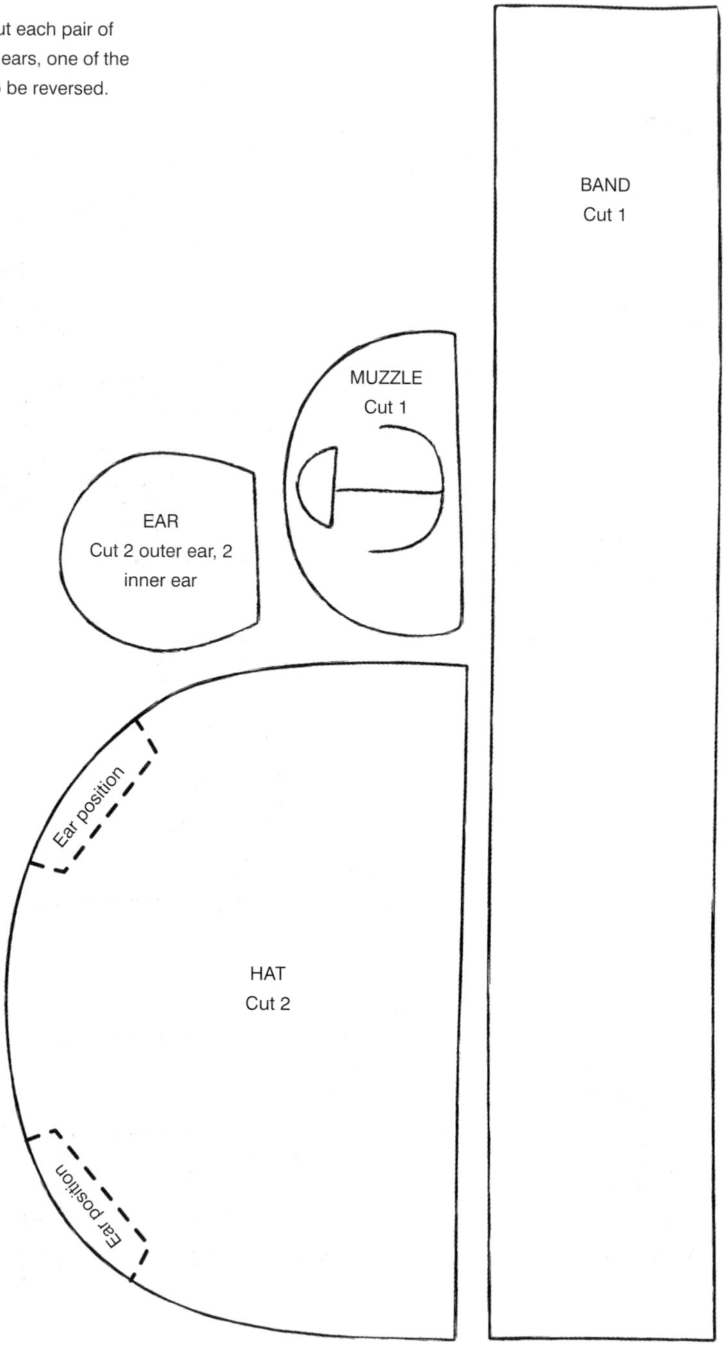

BAND
Cut 1

MUZZLE
Cut 1

EAR
Cut 2 outer ear, 2
inner ear

Ear position

HAT
Cut 2

Ear position

Toy Tidy

Use at 250%

When cutting out each pair of outer and inner ears, one of the pieces
needs to be reversed.

MOUSE
Cut ear as separate piece

DOG
Cut ear as
separate piece

RABBIT
Cut leg and inner
ear as separate
pieces

CAT
Cut muzzle and inner ears as
separate pieces

SHEEP
Cut head and legs as
separate pieces

PIG
Cut snout as separate piece

Use at 150%